Discovering 's

Copyright © 2023 by Alejandro Hugo Meyer

All rights reserved. No part of this book may be reproduced, stored in a retrieval system, or transmitted in any form or by any means, electronic, mechanical, photocopying, recording, or otherwise, without the prior written permission of the publisher.

The content provided in this book is for entertainment purposes only. It is not intended to serve as professional advice or guidance. Readers are advised to consult with appropriate professionals or authorities regarding specific concerns or topics discussed in this book. This book was created with the assistance of Artificial Intelligence technology.

The Jewel of Central America: Introducing Costa Rica 8

Echoes of the Past: Unraveling Costa Rica's Ancient History 11

Unveiling the Natural Wonders: Costa Rica's Breathtaking Landscapes 14

Pura Vida Lifestyle: Embracing the Essence of Costa Rican Culture 18

From Coast to Coast: Exploring Costa Rica's Stunning Beaches 22

Enchanting Rainforests: Discovering Costa Rica's Rich Biodiversity 26

A Symphony of Colors: The Vibrant Flora and Fauna of Costa Rica 29

Coffee Paradise: The Art and Science of Costa Rican Coffee 33

A World of Adventures: Thrill-seeking in Costa Rica 37

A Journey into the Past: Unearthing Costa Rica's Pre-Columbian Heritage 40

San José: The Capital City's Charms and Modern Marvels 43

Volcanoes Unleashed: Costa Rica's Fiery Peaks 46

Wildlife Wonderland: Exploring Costa Rica's National Parks 49

Tico Gastronomy: Savoring the Flavors of Costa Rican Cuisine 53

Mystical Waters: Costa Rica's Healing Hot Springs and Natural Spas 56

Sustainable Living: Costa Rica's Commitment to Eco-Tourism 59

Pacific Paradise: Delving into the Nicoya Peninsula 62

Carara National Park: Home to Scarlet Macaws and Exquisite Wildlife 65

A Taste of Paradise: Costa Rica's Exquisite Tropical Fruits 68

Monteverde Cloud Forest: An Enchanted Canopy Experience 71

Guanacaste: Sun, Sand, and Serenity on the Golden Coast 75

Quetzals and Clouds: The Resplendent Beauty of Savegre Valley 79

Tortuguero National Park: Witnessing the Miracle of Sea Turtles 83

From Sloths to Howler Monkeys: The Fascinating World of Costa Rican Wildlife 86

Manuel Antonio National Park: Where the Rainforest Meets the Sea 90

Bridging Past and Present: Costa Rica's Historic Landmarks 93

Osa Peninsula: A Pristine Wilderness Teeming with Life 97

Diving into the Deep Blue: Exploring Costa Rica's Underwater Treasures 101

Celestial Delights: Stargazing in Costa Rica's Dark Skies 104

Nicoya: Secrets of Longevity and Happiness 107

Hidden Gems: Costa Rica's Off-the-Beaten-Path Destinations 110

Arenal Volcano: Adventure and Relaxation in the Shadow of Fire 113

The Blue Zone of Costa Rica: A Fountain of Youth in the Nicoya Peninsula 117

Caribbean Bliss: Exploring Costa Rica's Lush East Coast 120

Rio Celeste: The Mystical Beauty of Costa Rica's Azure River 123

San Gerardo de Dota: Birdwatching Haven in the Cloud Forests 126

Surf's Up! Riding the Waves on Costa Rica's Legendary Beaches 130

Legends and Folklore: Tales from Costa Rica's Rich Oral Tradition 133

Flavors of the Earth: Costa Rica's Organic Farms and Sustainable Agriculture 137

A Journey into the Canopy: Zip-lining Adventures in Costa Rica 143

Indigenous Cultures: Celebrating Costa Rica's Native Heritage 147

Corcovado National Park: Untamed Wilderness on the Osa Peninsula 151

Orchid Paradise: Costa Rica's Spectacular Floral Kingdom 155

A Gastronomic Journey: Delving into Costa Rica's Culinary Delights 158

Wildlife Rehabilitation: Conservation Efforts in Costa Rica 162

Farewell, Costa Rica: Memories and Reflections on a Remarkable Journey 166

The Jewel of Central America: Introducing Costa Rica

Welcome to the mesmerizing world of Costa Rica, a country that stands as a shining gem in the heart of Central America. Known for its unparalleled natural beauty, warm and welcoming culture, and commitment to environmental conservation, Costa Rica is a true paradise that captivates the hearts of all who visit.

Nestled between the Pacific Ocean and the Caribbean Sea, Costa Rica is blessed with an astonishing diversity of landscapes. Picture yourself standing on a pristine white-sand beach, the gentle waves lapping at your feet as you gaze out at the crystal-clear turquoise waters. Inland, lush rainforests carpet the land, teeming with an awe-inspiring array of plant and animal species. Verdant mountains dotted with majestic volcanoes rise up to touch the sky, their peaks shrouded in mist. Costa Rica is a nature lover's dream come true, where every corner reveals a breathtaking panorama that will leave you speechless.

The country's commitment to conservation is nothing short of remarkable. With over 25% of its land designated as protected areas, Costa Rica has earned its reputation as an eco-tourism pioneer. It is home to an astonishing 5% of the world's biodiversity, making it one of the most biodiverse regions on the planet. From the elusive jaguars and playful monkeys to the vibrant toucans and dazzling hummingbirds, the wildlife here will enchant you at every turn.

But Costa Rica is not only defined by its natural wonders; it is also a nation steeped in rich cultural heritage. The people of Costa Rica, known as "Ticos," are renowned for their warm hospitality and the pervasive spirit of Pura Vida, which translates to "pure life." This philosophy embodies a laid-back and positive outlook on life, emphasizing the importance of enjoying the present moment and appreciating the simple joys that surround us. Ticos embrace visitors with open arms, sharing their traditions, music, and delectable cuisine, ensuring that every visitor feels like an honorary member of their vibrant community.

No exploration of Costa Rica would be complete without a taste of its world-famous coffee. Costa Rica's fertile volcanic soils and ideal climate provide the perfect conditions for cultivating some of the finest coffee beans in the world. Coffee production is deeply ingrained in the country's history and culture, and a visit to a coffee plantation offers a fascinating glimpse into the art and science behind this beloved beverage.

For those seeking adventure, Costa Rica is a playground of thrilling experiences. From zip-lining through the treetops of the rainforest to whitewater rafting down rushing rivers and surfing the renowned breaks along the coast, adrenaline junkies will find their nirvana here. Explore hidden waterfalls, hike through cloud forests, or embark on a nighttime turtle-watching expedition on the sandy shores. The possibilities for adventure are endless, ensuring that every day in Costa Rica is filled with excitement and unforgettable memories.

Costa Rica's capital, San José, provides a fascinating blend of old-world charm and modern sophistication. Explore its bustling markets, where vibrant colors and enticing aromas beckon you to discover unique handicrafts and fresh local produce. Immerse yourself in history as you wander through the elegant colonial architecture of its historic neighborhoods. And when the sun sets, the city comes alive with a vibrant nightlife scene, where music, dance, and laughter echo through the streets.

As you embark on your journey through Costa Rica, be prepared to witness the profound commitment to sustainability and environmental stewardship that permeates every aspect of life here. From renewable energy initiatives to organic farming practices, Costa Rica is a global leader in environmental conservation. It proudly maintains its status as one of the few countries in the world to have abolished its military, redirecting those funds towards education, healthcare, and the preservation of its natural treasures.

So pack your bags, open your heart, and prepare to be captivated by the beauty, warmth, and sheer magnificence of Costa Rica. Whether you seek tranquility in nature, thrilling adventures, cultural immersion, or simply the joy of embracing the Pura Vida lifestyle, Costa Rica will embrace you with open arms and leave an indelible mark on your soul. Get ready for an unforgettable journey through the jewel of Central America, where paradise awaits at every turn.

Echoes of the Past: Unraveling Costa Rica's Ancient History

Costa Rica's ancient history is a captivating tale of the early civilizations that inhabited this lush land long before the arrival of European explorers. It is a story of ancient cultures, remarkable achievements, and a deep connection to the natural world. As we delve into the depths of time, we discover the vibrant tapestry of Costa Rica's past, celebrating the resilience, ingenuity, and cultural heritage of its ancient peoples.

The earliest evidence of human presence in Costa Rica dates back thousands of years. Archaeological findings suggest that the region was first settled by hunter-gatherer groups around 10,000 BCE. These early inhabitants roamed the diverse landscapes, adapting to the challenges and bounties of their surroundings.

Over time, agriculture became central to the lives of Costa Rica's ancient peoples. By around 2,000 BCE, indigenous communities began cultivating crops such as maize, beans, squash, and cacao. This transition from a nomadic lifestyle to settled agricultural communities laid the foundation for the development of complex societies.

One of the most significant cultural regions in ancient Costa Rica was the Greater Nicoya Archaeological Region. Located in the northwestern part of the country, this area witnessed the rise of sophisticated societies characterized by distinct ceramic traditions and advanced agricultural practices. The people of this region created exquisite pottery, adorned with intricate designs and motifs that reflected their artistic sensibilities.

The presence of stone spheres in the Diquís Delta region remains an enigmatic aspect of ancient Costa Rican history. These perfectly round stone spheres, ranging in size from a few centimeters to over two meters in diameter, have puzzled archaeologists for years. The purpose and method of their creation still elude us, but they stand as a testament to the advanced craftsmanship and mathematical precision of the ancient inhabitants.

The ancient Costa Ricans developed complex cosmologies and engaged in rituals that honored nature and the spiritual realm. They believed in the interconnectedness of all things and sought harmony with the cosmos. Their spiritual worldview can be seen in the elaborate ceremonial centers and structures they built, such as those found at Guayabo de Turrialba and Las Mercedes. These architectural marvels reflected their societal organization and served as centers of community gatherings, ceremonies, and sacred rites.

The ancient Costa Ricans also excelled in various forms of craftsmanship. Goldsmithing was particularly notable, as they created intricate gold ornaments that reflected their status and adorned ceremonial attire. The craftsmanship extended to pottery, stone carving, and textile production, showcasing their artistic mastery and aesthetic sensibilities. Elaborate pottery vessels with detailed motifs and finely woven textiles testify to the skill and creativity of these ancient artisans.

Trade played a significant role in the lives of ancient Costa Ricans. Archaeological evidence suggests that the region was part of extensive regional trade networks, exchanging goods such as jade, obsidian, and other precious materials with neighboring cultures. This trade facilitated the exchange of ideas, technology, and cultural practices, contributing to the dynamic development of ancient Costa Rican societies.

The ancient history of Costa Rica is a testament to the enduring spirit of its people. Their ability to adapt, innovate, and create thriving communities in harmony with nature is truly remarkable. Today, we can marvel at their achievements and celebrate the profound cultural heritage they left behind.

As we explore the remnants of ancient Costa Rican civilizations, we are reminded of the deep roots that ground us and the connections we share with those who came before us. The rich tapestry of Costa Rica's ancient history inspires us to appreciate the natural wonders that surround us, embrace cultural diversity, and strive for harmony with the world around us.

In celebrating the ancient history of Costa Rica, we honor the ingenuity, creativity, and resilience of the ancient peoples who left their indelible mark on the land. Their legacy continues to shape the cultural fabric of Costa Rica, fostering a sense of pride and belonging for its present-day inhabitants.

Unveiling the Natural Wonders: Costa Rica's Breathtaking Landscapes

Prepare to embark on a journey through the enchanting landscapes of Costa Rica, where nature's wonders unfold in a symphony of breathtaking beauty. From pristine beaches and lush rainforests to majestic volcanoes and cascading waterfalls, this remarkable country offers a tapestry of landscapes that will leave you in awe.

Let's begin our exploration on the coast, where Costa Rica's stunning beaches beckon with their powdery sands and azure waters. Along the Pacific Coast, you'll discover a stretch of paradise known as the Nicoya Peninsula. This idyllic region boasts unspoiled beaches like Santa Teresa and Playa Conchal, where you can bask in the warm sun, swim in the crystal-clear waters, and indulge in the tranquil rhythms of beach life. On the Caribbean side, the beaches of Puerto Viejo and Cahuita offer a unique blend of laid-back vibes, vibrant reggae music, and the opportunity to snorkel amidst colorful coral reefs.

Venturing inland, you'll encounter the crown jewels of Costa Rica's natural wonders—the lush and verdant rainforests. The country's commitment to conservation has resulted in an impressive network of protected areas and national parks, where the dense canopies shelter an astounding array of flora and fauna. Explore the iconic Monteverde Cloud Forest Reserve, where misty trails lead you through a mystical world of hanging orchids, towering trees, and an abundance of wildlife. Traverse the trails of Corcovado National Park, one of the most biodiverse places on Earth, where scarlet macaws soar overhead, monkeys swing from branch to branch, and elusive jaguars prowl through the undergrowth.

In the heart of Costa Rica, you'll encounter the awe-inspiring Arenal Volcano, an active stratovolcano that stands as a majestic sentinel against the sky. Hike through the surrounding Arenal Volcano National Park to witness its volcanic activity, relax in natural hot springs fed by geothermal waters, and marvel at the magnificent La Fortuna Waterfall as it cascades down into a picturesque pool. The volcano's symmetrical cone and occasional eruptions create a dramatic backdrop for adventure and tranquility alike.

No exploration of Costa Rica's landscapes would be complete without immersing yourself in its network of pristine rivers and majestic waterfalls. The Rio Celeste, nestled within Tenorio Volcano National Park, offers an otherworldly experience with its stunning blue waters, a result of a unique chemical reaction. Witness the magic of La Paz Waterfall Gardens, where a series of cascades and lush gardens create an ethereal oasis. The sound of rushing water, the cool mist on your face, and the sight of nature's power in action will awaken a sense of wonder within you.

As you traverse Costa Rica's landscapes, keep your eyes peeled for the incredible array of wildlife that call this country home. Costa Rica is home to over 500,000 species, representing nearly 4% of the world's total biodiversity. Spot colorful toucans, playful monkeys, and vibrant tree frogs as you explore the treetops. Keep an eye out for the majestic quetzal, a sacred bird revered by ancient civilizations for its resplendent beauty. In Tortuguero National Park, witness the incredible journey of sea turtles as they make their way ashore to lay their eggs—a truly awe-inspiring spectacle of nature's cycles.

Costa Rica's landscapes aren't just visually breathtaking; they also offer a wealth of adventure and outdoor activities. For thrill-seekers, the country presents a playground of possibilities. Zip-line through the rainforest canopy, rappel down cascading waterfalls, or go whitewater rafting down rushing rivers that cut through dramatic gorges. Embark on a jungle safari, where you can spot wildlife from the comfort of a riverboat or enjoy a thrilling night hike to observe nocturnal creatures.

As you delve deeper into the landscapes of Costa Rica, you'll uncover hidden gems and off-the-beaten-path destinations that reveal the country's true essence. From the mystical cloud forests of San Gerardo de Dota to the hidden corners of the Osa Peninsula, where untouched wilderness and secluded beaches await, there's always a new discovery waiting to be made.

Costa Rica's landscapes are a testament to the country's commitment to environmental conservation. As you explore the natural wonders, you'll find a strong sense of sustainability and eco-consciousness ingrained in the fabric of the nation. Costa Rica has set a global example in eco-tourism, with initiatives that promote responsible travel and support local communities. By visiting this remarkable country, you become a part of this noble mission, contributing to the preservation of these landscapes for generations to come.

Prepare to be astonished, inspired, and humbled by the natural wonders that unfold before you in Costa Rica. This is a land where the harmony between humans and nature thrives, where breathtaking landscapes coexist with a commitment to conservation, and where the sheer beauty of the world reminds us of the preciousness of our planet. Open your heart, embrace the Pura Vida spirit, and let Costa Rica's landscapes ignite your sense of wonder and leave an indelible mark on your soul.

Pura Vida Lifestyle: Embracing the Essence of Costa Rican Culture

Welcome to the land of Pura Vida, where a vibrant culture rooted in warmth, simplicity, and appreciation for life awaits you. Costa Rica's Pura Vida lifestyle is not just a phrase; it's a way of being that permeates every aspect of the country's culture, making it a truly exceptional place to experience.

Pura Vida is more than just a greeting or a slogan; it's a philosophy that embodies a positive outlook on life. Translated as "pure life," Pura Vida represents an attitude of gratitude, resilience, and embracing the present moment. It's an invitation to slow down, savor the little things, and find joy in the simplest of pleasures.

One of the most remarkable aspects of the Pura Vida lifestyle is the warm and welcoming nature of the Costa Rican people, known as Ticos. Hospitality is deeply ingrained in the culture, and visitors are often treated like family. From the moment you arrive, you'll be greeted with genuine smiles, open hearts, and a genuine interest in making you feel at home. Whether you're exploring the bustling streets of San José or venturing into remote villages, you'll always find a friendly face ready to share their stories, traditions, and local customs.

Family is at the heart of Costa Rican culture, and the importance of strong familial bonds is evident in every aspect of life. Extended families often live in close proximity, creating a sense of community and support.

Family gatherings are treasured occasions, where generations come together to celebrate, share meals, and create lasting memories. This deep-rooted connection to family creates a sense of belonging and a strong support system that shapes the fabric of society.

Costa Rica's cultural heritage is rich and diverse, reflecting the country's historical influences and indigenous roots. The traditional music and dance of Costa Rica are a vibrant expression of its cultural identity. The marimba, a wooden xylophone-like instrument, takes center stage in many traditional musical performances, accompanied by lively folk dances that showcase the colorful costumes and intricate footwork of the performers.

Another integral part of Costa Rican culture is the strong connection to nature and the environment. With its lush rainforests, pristine beaches, and awe-inspiring landscapes, it's no wonder that Costa Ricans have a deep appreciation for the natural world around them. Environmental consciousness is deeply ingrained in the country's ethos, with Costa Rica being a global leader in sustainable practices and eco-tourism. The commitment to conservation is evident in the extensive network of national parks and protected areas that safeguard the country's biodiversity.

Cuisine is an integral part of any culture, and Costa Rica's gastronomy is a reflection of its vibrant heritage and agricultural abundance. Traditional Costa Rican cuisine is known for its simplicity, fresh ingredients, and hearty flavors. Gallo pinto, a combination of rice and black beans, is considered a national dish and is often enjoyed for breakfast. Succulent fruits like mangoes, papayas, and pineapples are abundant and add a burst of tropical sweetness to every meal. And let's not forget about the famous Costa Rican coffee, renowned for its high quality and smooth flavor. Coffee is not just a beverage but a cultural institution, with the daily ritual of sharing a cup of coffee fostering connections and conversations.

The arts and crafts of Costa Rica are another window into its cultural heritage. Talented artisans create intricate pottery, colorful textiles, and hand-carved wooden masks that showcase the country's artistic expressions. Whether you're browsing bustling markets or visiting artisan workshops, you'll find a treasure trove of unique and beautifully crafted souvenirs that reflect the soul of Costa Rican craftsmanship.

Pura Vida isn't just a concept limited to personal interactions—it extends to the way Costa Rica approaches societal issues. The country has long been a champion of peace and political stability, maintaining a proud tradition of democracy and fostering a society that values equality, education, and social progress. Costa Rica abolished its military in 1949, redirecting resources towards education, healthcare, and the preservation of its natural heritage. This commitment to peace and progress has earned Costa Rica international acclaim as a beacon of stability and progress in the region.

Immersing yourself in the Pura Vida lifestyle means embracing a slower pace, being present in the moment, and finding joy in the simple pleasures of life. It's about connecting with nature, celebrating community, and cultivating a positive and grateful mindset. From savoring a cup of rich Costa Rican coffee to sharing laughter with newfound friends, every day in Costa Rica is an opportunity to embody the essence of Pura Vida and experience the transformative power of embracing a vibrant and joyous way of life.

Costa Rica's Pura Vida lifestyle is an invitation to rediscover the beauty of simplicity, the power of human connection, and the joy of living in harmony with nature. It's a cultural tapestry woven with warmth, gratitude, and resilience—a celebration of life in its purest form. So, embrace the essence of Costa Rican culture, open your heart to the Pura Vida way of life, and let the magic of this extraordinary country leave an indelible mark on your soul.

From Coast to Coast: Exploring Costa Rica's Stunning Beaches

Welcome to a coastal paradise like no other—Costa Rica, a country renowned for its stunning beaches that stretch along both the Pacific Ocean and the Caribbean Sea. From pristine white sands to secluded coves and vibrant coastal towns, Costa Rica's beaches offer a tapestry of beauty and tranquility that will leave you captivated.

Let's begin our coastal journey on the Pacific side, where a treasure trove of breathtaking beaches awaits. Tamarindo, located in the province of Guanacaste, is a popular destination known for its golden sands, clear waters, and vibrant surf scene. Here, you can catch the perfect wave, take a leisurely beach stroll, or witness a breathtaking sunset that paints the sky in hues of pink and gold.

Further south lies Manuel Antonio, a coastal gem nestled within a national park. This idyllic beach destination offers a unique blend of natural beauty and abundant wildlife. Imagine relaxing on pristine beaches framed by lush rainforest, while capuchin monkeys frolic in the trees above and colorful parrots soar through the sky. Exploring the trails of Manuel Antonio National Park will reveal hidden beaches, natural pools, and the chance to encounter fascinating wildlife up close.

For those seeking a taste of the exotic Caribbean, Costa Rica's eastern coast offers a different kind of coastal experience. Puerto Viejo de Talamanca, a laid-back beach town, exudes a bohemian charm that invites visitors to slow down and embrace the vibrant reggae-infused rhythms of the Caribbean. Here, you can relax on pristine beaches, immerse yourself in the local Afro-Caribbean culture, and savor the flavors of traditional cuisine influenced by African, Indigenous, and European traditions.

As we journey north along the Caribbean coast, we encounter the hidden gem of Cahuita. This small coastal village is home to Cahuita National Park, a protected marine reserve that boasts breathtaking coral reefs and vibrant underwater ecosystems. Snorkelers and divers will be mesmerized by the kaleidoscope of colors and diverse marine life that thrives within the park's boundaries.

Back on the Pacific coast, the Nicoya Peninsula offers a paradise of serene beaches and untouched landscapes. Santa Teresa, a popular surf destination, enchants visitors with its pristine white sands, turquoise waters, and laid-back atmosphere. Surfers from around the world flock to its renowned breaks, while those seeking relaxation can indulge in yoga retreats or simply soak up the sun's warm embrace.

In the Gulf of Papagayo, the beach resorts of Playa Hermosa and Playas del Coco provide the perfect blend of natural beauty and modern amenities. Picture yourself lounging on palm-fringed shores, sipping a refreshing cocktail as you watch sailboats glide across the glistening waters. The region's calm waters are ideal for swimming, snorkeling, and exploring the abundant marine life that inhabits the vibrant coral reefs.

Venturing further south, we arrive at the Osa Peninsula, a true wilderness where untouched beaches meet dense rainforests. Drake Bay and Corcovado National Park offer a rugged and untamed coastal experience, where you can immerse yourself in pristine nature and encounter wildlife such as dolphins, sea turtles, and even humpback whales during migration season. Here, you can trek through the jungle, kayak along winding mangrove forests, or simply unwind on secluded beaches that feel like your own private sanctuary.

Costa Rica's beaches are not just about sun, sand, and surf—they are also gateways to a world of adventure. Along the coast, you can embark on thrilling activities such as kayaking through hidden mangroves, embarking on a deep-sea fishing expedition, or exploring the underwater wonders through scuba diving or snorkeling. The rich marine biodiversity and vibrant coral reefs offer endless opportunities for exploration and discovery.

What sets Costa Rica's beaches apart is not just their natural beauty, but also the country's unwavering commitment to environmental conservation. Many of the beach areas are protected, ensuring that these coastal ecosystems thrive for generations to come. Costa Rica's dedication to sustainable tourism practices promotes the preservation of marine life, protection of delicate ecosystems, and the education of visitors about the importance of responsible travel.

So, whether you seek relaxation, exhilaration, or a deep connection with nature, Costa Rica's stunning beaches offer an invitation to immerse yourself in the sheer beauty and serenity of the coastal landscapes. Let the rhythmic sounds of the waves, the warmth of the sun on your skin, and the endless stretches of pristine sands rejuvenate your spirit and leave you with cherished memories of a coastal paradise unlike any other.

Enchanting Rainforests: Discovering Costa Rica's Rich Biodiversity

Prepare to embark on a captivating journey through the enchanting rainforests of Costa Rica, where a world of astounding biodiversity awaits. Nestled between the Pacific Ocean and the Caribbean Sea, this verdant paradise is home to some of the most diverse and vibrant ecosystems on the planet.

Costa Rica's rainforests are a living testament to the country's commitment to environmental conservation. With over 25% of its land protected in national parks and reserves, the preservation of these precious ecosystems is a top priority. This dedication has resulted in Costa Rica being recognized as one of the most biodiverse regions in the world, housing an astonishing 5% of Earth's total biodiversity.

As you venture into the depths of Costa Rica's rainforests, you'll find yourself immersed in a symphony of colors, sounds, and scents. Towering trees, draped with cascading vines and vibrant epiphytes, create a mesmerizing canopy that filters sunlight and nurtures an abundance of life below. Sunlight dapples the forest floor, illuminating a carpet of lush ferns, delicate orchids, and an array of flowering plants that paint the landscape with a riot of hues.

The rainforests of Costa Rica are teeming with an incredible diversity of wildlife, showcasing the interconnectedness of species within these complex ecosystems. Monkeys swing effortlessly through the treetops, their playful antics adding a touch of joy to the surroundings. Sloths lazily cling to branches, their slow movements blending seamlessly with the unhurried pace of the rainforest. Vibrant toucans and scarlet macaws flash their brilliant plumage, while elusive jaguars and ocelots silently navigate the undergrowth.

One of the most remarkable inhabitants of the rainforest is the resplendent quetzal, a bird revered by ancient civilizations for its breathtaking beauty. Its iridescent green plumage and long, flowing tail feathers make it a symbol of mystique and wonder. Spotting this elusive creature in its natural habitat is a privilege that few are fortunate enough to experience.

The rivers that flow through Costa Rica's rainforests offer a lifeline to the intricate web of life within these lush ecosystems. They provide a source of nourishment for the flora and fauna, creating thriving habitats for a multitude of species. Exploring these rivers by boat or kayak allows you to witness the intricate ballet of nature firsthand. Glide silently along the waterways and observe the diverse array of aquatic life, from colorful fish darting beneath the surface to crocodiles basking in the sun along the riverbanks.

Costa Rica's rainforests are also home to a myriad of fascinating insects and amphibians. Leafcutter ants march tirelessly along their intricate trails, carrying leaf fragments many times their size. Dart frogs, with their vibrant hues and intricate patterns, add a touch of artistic beauty to the forest floor. These tiny creatures serve as a reminder that even the smallest inhabitants play a crucial role in maintaining the delicate balance of the rainforest ecosystem.

Exploring the rainforests of Costa Rica isn't just about witnessing nature's splendor; it's also about connecting with the rhythm of the jungle and embracing its therapeutic power. The air is alive with the soothing sounds of chirping birds, buzzing insects, and the gentle rustle of leaves. The scent of damp earth and exotic flowers fills your lungs, rejuvenating your spirit and reconnecting you with the natural world.

Costa Rica's commitment to conservation goes beyond protecting the rainforests; it also encompasses a dedication to sustainable practices and eco-tourism. Many of the country's national parks and reserves offer carefully planned trails and educational programs that allow visitors to explore and appreciate the rainforest while minimizing their impact on the environment. By promoting responsible travel, Costa Rica ensures that these captivating ecosystems are preserved for future generations to experience and cherish.

In the rainforests of Costa Rica, you'll discover a profound sense of wonder, a deep appreciation for nature's intricate beauty, and a renewed understanding of our role as custodians of the Earth. The biodiversity that thrives within these enchanting habitats is a testament to the resilience and interconnectedness of life itself. So, step into the embrace of Costa Rica's rainforests, let their beauty envelop you, and embark on a journey that will forever transform your relationship with the natural world.

A Symphony of Colors: The Vibrant Flora and Fauna of Costa Rica

Welcome to a world of unparalleled beauty, where a symphony of colors dances across the landscapes of Costa Rica. From vibrant flora to diverse fauna, this tropical paradise is a living canvas that celebrates the wonders of nature in the most captivating way.

Costa Rica's astonishing biodiversity is a result of its unique geographical location and varied ecosystems. It serves as a bridge between North and South America, allowing for the blending of species from both continents. This convergence has created a rich tapestry of life, making Costa Rica one of the most biodiverse regions on Earth.

Let's start our exploration with the flora that adorns the landscapes of Costa Rica. From the moment you set foot in this remarkable country, you'll be surrounded by an explosion of colors. Orchids, with their delicate and intricate blooms, can be found in countless varieties, creating a kaleidoscope of shades and patterns. The national flower of Costa Rica, the guaria morada, showcases stunning purple petals that symbolize the beauty and resilience of the nation.

The rainforests of Costa Rica are a botanical wonderland, with towering trees reaching towards the heavens and an understory filled with lush ferns, bromeliads, and mosses. Epiphytes, such as the colorful bromeliad known as the "air plant," thrive by attaching themselves to trees and absorbing moisture from the air. These botanical treasures create a sense of enchantment as you stroll through the verdant pathways of the rainforest.

As we delve deeper into the fauna of Costa Rica, prepare to be awestruck by the incredible diversity of wildlife that calls this country home. Costa Rica boasts over 500,000 species, representing nearly 4% of the world's total biodiversity. It's a haven for nature enthusiasts, photographers, and wildlife lovers alike.

Monkeys swing through the treetops, their acrobatic antics adding a playful energy to the rainforest. The howler monkeys make their presence known with their powerful vocalizations that resonate through the canopy. Spider monkeys display their remarkable agility, effortlessly moving from branch to branch. Capuchin monkeys, with their expressive faces and lively demeanor, capture the hearts of all who encounter them.

Sloths, the embodiment of tranquility, hang serenely from branches, moving at their own leisurely pace. These gentle creatures are a testament to the unhurried rhythms of the rainforest and remind us to slow down and appreciate the beauty of stillness.

The avian inhabitants of Costa Rica are equally captivating. Over 900 species of birds have been recorded here, ranging from tiny hummingbirds to majestic raptors. The resplendent quetzal, with its emerald green plumage and long, flowing tail feathers, is a symbol of beauty and mystique. Toucans, with their vibrant beaks and playful personalities, bring a touch of whimsy to the treetops. Scarlet macaws, with their brilliant red, blue, and yellow feathers, adorn the skies and add a splash of vivid color to the rainforest canopy.

In Costa Rica's coastal areas, the marine ecosystems are teeming with life. Snorkeling or diving along the coral reefs reveals a dazzling array of colorful fish, graceful sea turtles, and delicate seahorses. The waters off the Pacific coast are visited by migrating humpback whales, while dolphins playfully frolic in the surf. Costa Rica's commitment to marine conservation ensures that these underwater ecosystems remain vibrant and thriving for generations to come.

But the vibrant flora and fauna of Costa Rica aren't confined to the rainforests and coastlines alone. From the misty cloud forests of Monteverde to the mangrove swamps of Tortuguero, each ecosystem harbors its own unique cast of characters. Dart frogs, with their vibrant colors and intricate patterns, add an artistic touch to the forest floor. The elusive jaguars and ocelots, emblematic of wild beauty and strength, remind us of the hidden wonders that lie within the dense foliage.

Costa Rica's dedication to environmental conservation and sustainable practices ensures the preservation of this incredible biodiversity. It's a testament to the country's commitment to being a responsible steward of its natural treasures.

As you immerse yourself in the symphony of colors that unfolds in Costa Rica, you'll witness the beauty and interconnectedness of life. Each vibrant hue, each delicate petal, and each unique creature contribute to the harmonious composition of the country's ecosystems. Costa Rica's commitment to preserving this remarkable biodiversity is a gift not only to the nation but to the world.

So, open your eyes to the vibrant palette of Costa Rica, where every corner reveals a new burst of color and every encounter with its fauna leaves an indelible imprint on your soul. Celebrate the breathtaking flora and fauna of this tropical paradise, and let the symphony of colors captivate your heart as you explore the wonders of Costa Rica.

Coffee Paradise: The Art and Science of Costa Rican Coffee

Step into a world of rich aromas, exquisite flavors, and a centuries-old tradition that has shaped Costa Rican culture—the world of Costa Rican coffee. Nestled within the lush landscapes and fertile volcanic soils, Costa Rica has earned a well-deserved reputation for producing some of the finest coffee beans in the world. Prepare to embark on a journey that unveils the art and science behind this beloved beverage.

Costa Rica's coffee industry traces its roots back to the early 19th century when coffee cultivation began to flourish. Today, coffee production remains an integral part of the country's identity and economy. The ideal climate, high altitude, and volcanic soils create the perfect conditions for cultivating superior Arabica coffee beans, known for their exceptional quality and distinct flavors.

The process of cultivating coffee in Costa Rica is a labor of love, blending tradition with scientific expertise. Coffee plantations, known as fincas, dot the landscape, their terraced slopes covered with row upon row of coffee plants. The cultivation process begins with careful selection of the coffee varietals, taking into account factors such as altitude, climate, and soil composition.

The coffee plants are meticulously nurtured, with farmers monitoring factors such as water levels, sunlight exposure, and pest control. They work in harmony with nature, implementing sustainable practices that minimize the environmental impact and ensure the long-term viability of the coffee crops. Costa Rica's commitment to sustainable coffee production has earned it recognition as one of the leading countries in environmentally friendly practices within the coffee industry.

Harvesting the coffee cherries is a delicate task that requires precision and timing. Skilled workers carefully handpick the ripe cherries, selecting only those at the peak of maturity. This selective harvesting process ensures that only the highest-quality beans make their way into the final product. It is a labor-intensive process that reflects the dedication and passion of the farmers.

Once harvested, the coffee cherries undergo a meticulous process to extract the beans. Traditional methods involve removing the pulp through a process called wet milling, followed by fermentation and washing to remove any residual pulp. The beans are then dried naturally under the sun or through mechanical means, allowing them to reach the optimal moisture content.

The final step in the journey from bean to cup is the roasting process, where the flavors and aromas of the coffee are unlocked. Costa Rican coffee roasters take great pride in their craft, carefully controlling the temperature and duration of the roasting process to bring out the unique characteristics of each coffee batch. Whether it's a light roast that preserves the subtle nuances or a dark roast that intensifies the flavors, the artistry of the roasting process elevates Costa Rican coffee to new heights.

Costa Rican coffee is known for its remarkable flavor profiles, ranging from bright and fruity to chocolatey and nutty. The distinct microclimates within the country's different coffee-growing regions contribute to the unique flavor profiles found in each cup. The Tarrazú region, for example, produces coffee with a bright acidity and notes of citrus and berries, while the Central Valley region yields beans with balanced flavors and a hint of chocolate.

The commitment to quality is further exemplified through certifications such as "Café de Costa Rica" and the designation of origin "Café de Tarrazú." These labels ensure that consumers are enjoying coffee of the highest standards, produced with adherence to strict quality control measures and the traditional practices that have been passed down through generations.

For coffee enthusiasts, a visit to Costa Rica offers an opportunity to delve deeper into the world of coffee. Coffee tours and tastings allow visitors to trace the journey of the beans from the plantation to the cup, gaining insight into the intricate process and experiencing the richness of Costa Rican coffee firsthand. You can witness the care and precision that goes into every step, from the cultivation to the final brewing.

Costa Rican coffee is not just a beverage; it's a cultural institution—a source of pride and a reflection of the nation's heritage. The daily ritual of sharing a cup of coffee fosters connections, conversations, and moments of pure enjoyment. It's a symbol of warmth, hospitality, and the laid-back lifestyle that embodies the essence of Costa Rica.

So, savor each sip, let the flavors dance on your palate, and celebrate the art and science of Costa Rican coffee. Immerse yourself in the world of this beloved beverage, and let its richness and depth awaken your senses as you embrace the coffee paradise that is Costa Rica.

A World of Adventures: Thrill-seeking in Costa Rica

Welcome to a playground for thrill-seekers, where adrenaline rushes and unforgettable experiences await at every turn—Costa Rica. This remarkable country offers a world of adventures that will leave you exhilarated, inspired, and craving for more. From heart-pounding activities in the wild to daring feats in the air and water, Costa Rica is a haven for those seeking an adrenaline-fueled escapade. Let's start our journey with the natural wonders that provide the backdrop for these exhilarating adventures. Costa Rica's lush rainforests and towering volcanoes set the stage for incredible hiking and trekking expeditions. Strap on your boots and venture into the mystical cloud forests of Monteverde or the awe-inspiring landscapes of Arenal Volcano National Park. Traverse rugged trails, cross hanging bridges, and be rewarded with breathtaking views and a sense of accomplishment that comes from conquering nature's challenges.

For those who prefer to take to the skies, Costa Rica offers a variety of thrilling experiences that will make your heart soar. Zip-lining through the rainforest canopy is a must-do adventure that allows you to glide effortlessly above the treetops, gaining a unique perspective of the vibrant ecosystem below. Feel the rush of adrenaline as you zip from one platform to another, surrounded by the sights and sounds of the jungle. Some zip-line tours even offer the opportunity to rappel down towering waterfalls, adding an extra element of excitement to the experience.

If you're looking for a truly unforgettable adventure, consider embarking on a skydiving expedition. Leap from a plane and freefall through the crisp, blue skies before your parachute opens, offering a breathtaking panorama of Costa Rica's stunning landscapes below. Whether it's soaring over the coastlines, rainforests, or majestic volcanoes, skydiving in Costa Rica is an experience that will forever be etched in your memory.

Costa Rica's abundant waterways present a myriad of thrilling opportunities for water enthusiasts. Brace yourself for the exhilaration of white-water rafting down rushing rivers, navigating through exhilarating rapids as the water churns and splashes around you. The Pacuare River, renowned for its world-class rapids, offers an adrenaline-pumping adventure set against the backdrop of pristine rainforest scenery.

Surfing aficionados flock to Costa Rica's Pacific coast, where world-class breaks provide endless opportunities to ride the waves. Whether you're a seasoned pro or a beginner eager to catch your first wave, the beaches of Tamarindo, Santa Teresa, and Dominical offer ideal conditions for an unforgettable surfing experience. Feel the rush of adrenaline as you paddle into the lineup, ride the curling waves, and experience the sheer joy of harnessing the power of the ocean.

Diving and snorkeling in Costa Rica's coastal waters is like entering a vibrant underwater wonderland. The country's rich marine biodiversity reveals itself as you dive beneath the surface, with colorful coral reefs, mesmerizing schools of tropical fish, and encounters with graceful sea turtles and majestic manta rays. Dive sites such as Cocos Island and Cano Island are world-renowned for their exceptional diving experiences, where you can explore underwater caves, encounter sharks, and marvel at the teeming marine life.

For the ultimate adrenaline rush, consider canyoning—a thrilling activity that involves rappelling down cascading waterfalls and plunging into crystal-clear pools. Descend through the rugged canyons of Costa Rica, feeling the rush of water against your skin as you navigate the natural obstacles. It's a heart-pounding adventure that combines the beauty of the natural surroundings with an element of daring. As you indulge in these adrenaline-fueled adventures, rest assured that Costa Rica prioritizes safety and responsible tourism. Experienced guides and tour operators adhere to strict safety protocols, ensuring that you can enjoy your adventures with peace of mind.

Costa Rica's commitment to eco-tourism and sustainable practices extends to adventure tourism as well. The country's dedication to environmental conservation ensures that these thrilling activities are carried out in a manner that minimizes impact on the ecosystems. Whether it's through waste management, wildlife protection, or the promotion of responsible behavior, Costa Rica aims to preserve its natural heritage while offering unforgettable adventures.

So, gear up, get ready to push your limits, and embark on a world of adventures in Costa Rica. Whether you're soaring through the air, conquering challenging trails, or diving into the depths of the ocean, let the thrill of these experiences ignite your spirit and leave you with memories that will last a lifetime. Costa Rica is a land of excitement and adventure, inviting you to embrace the thrill-seeking side of life and revel in the exhilaration of this incredible country.

A Journey into the Past: Unearthing Costa Rica's Pre-Columbian Heritage

Step back in time and embark on a fascinating journey into Costa Rica's pre-Columbian past, where ancient civilizations once thrived and left behind a rich and intriguing legacy. Unearthing Costa Rica's pre-Columbian heritage is like piecing together a captivating puzzle, revealing the remarkable history and cultural heritage of this vibrant land.

Long before the arrival of European explorers, indigenous peoples inhabited the region that is now known as Costa Rica. These diverse cultures developed unique societies, creating intricate systems of governance, art, and religious practices that shaped the fabric of their existence. Exploring their ancient sites and artifacts offers a glimpse into their way of life and their deep connection to the land.

One of the most iconic archaeological sites in Costa Rica is Guayabo de Turrialba. This ancient city, located in the Turrialba Valley, dates back over 2,000 years and provides valuable insights into the region's pre-Columbian civilizations. The site features stone-paved roads, plazas, aqueducts, and even a sophisticated water drainage system—a testament to the engineering skills and advanced urban planning of the ancient inhabitants.

The mysterious stone spheres of Costa Rica, found mainly in the Diquis Delta region, are another intriguing remnant of the past. These perfectly spherical stones, some weighing several tons, have puzzled archaeologists for centuries. The purpose and methods of their creation remain a subject of debate, but their significance as cultural artifacts is undeniable. Today, the stone spheres are recognized as a UNESCO World Heritage Site and a symbol of Costa Rica's pre-Columbian heritage.

Costa Rica's pre-Columbian cultures also expressed their creativity and beliefs through intricate art and craftsmanship. Jade, a precious stone revered for its beauty and symbolic importance, was meticulously carved into intricate pendants, beads, and figurines. Gold, too, held great significance and was fashioned into ornate jewelry and ceremonial objects. These exquisite artifacts, discovered in archaeological sites and ancient burial grounds, showcase the artistry and craftsmanship of the pre-Columbian civilizations.

The indigenous peoples of Costa Rica were deeply connected to nature, and their belief systems were intertwined with the natural world around them. Many of their rituals and ceremonies revolved around agriculture, fertility, and the changing seasons. They worshipped deities associated with natural elements such as the sun, moon, and rain, seeking harmony and balance in their interactions with the environment.

Costa Rica's pre-Columbian heritage is not confined to grand archaeological sites and artifacts—it lives on in the traditions and customs of the indigenous communities that continue to thrive today. The BriBri, Boruca, and Guaymí are just a few of the indigenous groups that have preserved their cultural practices, language, and spiritual beliefs. Through their vibrant festivals, traditional dances, and intricate handicrafts, they celebrate their ancestral heritage and keep their traditions alive.

Exploring Costa Rica's pre-Columbian heritage is a journey of discovery and appreciation for the enduring legacies of the past. It is a testament to the resilience and ingenuity of the indigenous peoples who forged a connection with the land and left an indelible mark on Costa Rica's cultural identity.

As you delve into this rich tapestry of history, immerse yourself in the stories of the past, and let the remnants of ancient civilizations transport you to a time of mystery and wonder. Costa Rica's pre-Columbian heritage is a treasure trove of knowledge and beauty, and by celebrating and understanding it, we gain a deeper appreciation for the diverse cultural heritage that shapes this extraordinary country.

San José: The Capital City's Charms and Modern Marvels

Welcome to San José, the vibrant capital city of Costa Rica—a cultural hub where history meets modernity and charm permeates every corner. Nestled in the heart of the Central Valley, San José offers a captivating blend of traditional architecture, lively markets, and a burgeoning arts scene, making it a destination that captivates visitors with its unique allure.

As you wander through the streets of San José, you'll be greeted by a delightful mix of colonial and contemporary architecture. The historic district of Barrio Amón showcases elegant mansions adorned with ornate facades and intricate wrought-iron balconies—a reminder of the city's colonial past. Stroll through the narrow streets, lined with colorful buildings, and soak up the ambiance of a bygone era.

San José is a city that celebrates its rich cultural heritage, and museums play a pivotal role in preserving and showcasing the country's history and art. The National Museum, housed in a former military fortress, offers a journey through Costa Rica's past, with exhibits that highlight the country's archaeological treasures, pre-Columbian artifacts, and colonial history. The Museum of Contemporary Art and Design showcases the works of local and international artists, providing a platform for the thriving art scene in San José.

One of the city's most iconic landmarks is the Teatro Nacional, a majestic theater that stands as a testament to Costa Rica's appreciation for the performing arts.

Admire the neoclassical architecture, adorned with intricate sculptures and stunning murals, as you step into a world of culture and creativity. The theater hosts a variety of performances, including ballets, concerts, and theater productions, showcasing the immense talent and passion of Costa Rican artists.

For those seeking a taste of local flavors and vibrant markets, a visit to the Mercado Central is a must. This bustling market is a sensory delight, with stalls brimming with tropical fruits, aromatic spices, and fresh seafood. Immerse yourself in the vibrant atmosphere, interact with the friendly vendors, and sample traditional dishes such as casados, gallo pinto, and empanadas. The Mercado Central offers a true glimpse into Costa Rican daily life and the culinary traditions that define the country's gastronomy.

San José is also a city that embraces green spaces and natural beauty. Parque Metropolitano La Sabana, the city's largest urban park, offers a tranquil oasis amidst the urban bustle. Take a leisurely stroll or enjoy a picnic on the expansive green lawns, surrounded by towering trees and vibrant flower beds. The park also houses the National Stadium, a state-of-the-art sports venue that hosts international events and serves as a hub for sports enthusiasts.

Art enthusiasts will find solace in San José's burgeoning art scene. The city is home to numerous galleries and art spaces that showcase the works of local artists, from contemporary paintings and sculptures to experimental installations. The city's art scene is dynamic and ever-evolving, reflecting the creative spirit and diversity of Costa Rican culture.

As the sun sets, San José comes alive with a vibrant nightlife. The city offers a range of entertainment options, from trendy bars and clubs to cozy cafés and live music venues. Join the locals and visitors as they dance to the rhythms of salsa, merengue, and reggaeton, or simply relax with a delicious cup of Costa Rican coffee and immerse yourself in the buzzing energy of the city.

San José is not just a gateway to Costa Rica's natural wonders—it is a destination in itself, a city that invites you to discover its charms and immerse yourself in its vibrant culture. So, embrace the modern marvels and historical gems of San José, and let the city's charm and allure captivate your heart as you explore the beating pulse of Costa Rica's capital.

Volcanoes Unleashed: Costa Rica's Fiery Peaks

Prepare to witness the raw power and mesmerizing beauty of Costa Rica's fiery peaks as we delve into the world of volcanoes. Nestled within the country's diverse landscapes, these majestic volcanoes are a testament to the geological wonders that have shaped Costa Rica's extraordinary natural heritage.

Costa Rica is home to more than 200 volcanic formations, with a handful of them classified as active or potentially active. These towering giants, both awe-inspiring and humbling, have played a significant role in shaping the country's landscapes, culture, and even its fertile soils.

Arenal Volcano, one of Costa Rica's most renowned volcanoes, rises majestically in the northern region. Its symmetrical cone, adorned with lush vegetation, creates a picture-perfect backdrop for any traveler seeking volcanic adventures. Arenal was active until 2010 when it entered a resting phase, but its legacy of fiery eruptions and glowing lava flows remains etched in the memories of those who witnessed its power.

Poás Volcano, located in the Central Valley, offers a different kind of volcanic experience. Its main crater is one of the largest in the world, with intermittent geyser-like eruptions that create an awe-inspiring spectacle. Visitors to Poás can gaze into the turquoise acidic crater lake and witness the fumaroles, or steam vents, emanating from its depths. The surrounding Poás Volcano National Park provides a serene setting for exploration, with hiking trails that wind through cloud forests and reveal stunning panoramic views.

Turrialba Volcano, situated east of San José, is an active volcano that has recently reawakened, capturing the attention of adventurers and scientists alike. Though its activity level fluctuates, Turrialba offers a glimpse into the dynamic nature of Costa Rica's volcanic landscape. Its ash emissions and occasional explosive eruptions serve as a reminder of the powerful forces beneath the Earth's surface.

In addition to these iconic volcanoes, Costa Rica boasts a wealth of other volcanic wonders. Rincón de la Vieja Volcano, with its bubbling mud pots, hot springs, and steaming fumaroles, creates an otherworldly experience for visitors. Irazú Volcano, the highest volcano in Costa Rica, rewards hikers with breathtaking views from its summit, where on a clear day, both the Pacific and Caribbean coasts can be seen simultaneously.

The volcanic activity in Costa Rica not only shapes the physical landscape but also contributes to the country's biodiversity and fertile soils. The mineral-rich volcanic ash enriches the earth, supporting lush forests, vibrant flora, and abundant wildlife. These volcanic ecosystems provide a haven for countless species, showcasing the intricate balance between geological forces and the delicate web of life.

Costa Rica's volcanoes offer more than just awe-inspiring vistas—they provide opportunities for adventure and exploration. Hiking trails lead intrepid adventurers through dense rainforests, across lava fields, and to volcanic craters. The journey to the summit of a volcano is an experience like no other, rewarding those who persevere with panoramic views and a deep sense of accomplishment.

For the adrenaline seekers, volcano boarding down Cerro Negro in neighboring Nicaragua offers an exhilarating descent down the ash-covered slopes. Strap on a protective suit, hop on a specially designed board, and feel the rush as you slide down the volcanic scree at thrilling speeds.

Costa Rica's commitment to the preservation and conservation of its volcanic areas is evident in the establishment of national parks and protected areas surrounding these geological wonders. These measures ensure the protection of the fragile ecosystems, while also providing opportunities for educational programs, research, and sustainable tourism practices.

So, venture into the realm of Costa Rica's fiery peaks, and let the volcanoes ignite your sense of wonder and adventure. Explore their rugged beauty, marvel at their power, and appreciate the intricate interplay between geological forces and the natural world. Costa Rica's volcanoes are not just geological features—they are testament to the remarkable forces that have shaped the country and continue to inspire awe in all who encounter them.

Wildlife Wonderland: Exploring Costa Rica's National Parks

Welcome to a wildlife wonderland, where Costa Rica's national parks offer an unrivaled opportunity to immerse yourself in the incredible biodiversity of this vibrant country. Spanning from coast to coast, these protected areas are a testament to Costa Rica's commitment to environmental conservation and serve as havens for a myriad of species, making them a paradise for nature lovers and wildlife enthusiasts.

Manuel Antonio National Park, located on the Pacific coast, is a jewel of Costa Rica's national park system. This tropical paradise combines pristine beaches with dense rainforests, creating a haven for a stunning array of wildlife. As you explore its trails, you may encounter playful white-faced capuchin monkeys swinging through the trees, three-toed sloths leisurely moving through the canopy, and vibrant toucans soaring above. The park's diverse ecosystems also support an impressive marine life, with snorkeling and diving opportunities to encounter colorful fish and graceful sea turtles.

Tortuguero National Park, on the Caribbean coast, is a haven for turtle enthusiasts. Its extensive network of canals, lagoons, and wetlands provides critical nesting grounds for endangered sea turtles, including the majestic green turtle and the iconic leatherback turtle. Witnessing a mother turtle laying her eggs or observing the hatchlings making their way to the ocean is a truly unforgettable experience. The park's lush rainforests are also home to howler monkeys, jaguars, and an astonishing variety of bird species, making it a wildlife enthusiast's dream.

Corcovado National Park, located on the Osa Peninsula, is often referred to as the crown jewel of Costa Rica's national park system. It boasts one of the most biodiverse regions on the planet, with over 500 species of trees, 140 species of mammals, and 400 species of birds. Jaguars, tapirs, and scarlet macaws are just a few of the charismatic species that call this park home. Hiking through its pristine rainforests, listening to the symphony of wildlife, and witnessing the interconnectedness of species is an awe-inspiring experience.

Monteverde Cloud Forest Reserve, nestled in the misty mountains of the country's central region, is a haven for biodiversity and a sanctuary for rare and endemic species. As you explore its ethereal trails, you'll be enchanted by the mystical atmosphere created by the clouds that hover amidst the lush foliage. Keep an eye out for the elusive resplendent quetzal, a symbol of beauty and mystique, as well as the vibrant hummingbirds that flit among the flowers. The cloud forest is also home to a vast array of orchids, bromeliads, and ferns, creating a botanical wonderland.

La Amistad International Park, shared with neighboring Panama, is a UNESCO World Heritage Site that encompasses rugged mountains, deep valleys, and pristine rainforests. This vast wilderness is home to numerous endangered species, including the iconic harpy eagle and the elusive jaguar. Exploring this untamed landscape is a true adventure, offering opportunities for trekking, bird-watching, and immersing oneself in the untouched beauty of nature.

Costa Rica's commitment to conservation extends beyond individual parks—over 25% of the country's land is protected within a network of national parks, reserves, and wildlife refuges. This dedication has led to Costa Rica being recognized as one of the most biodiverse countries in the world, with approximately 6% of the world's terrestrial species found within its borders.

Beyond the flagship parks mentioned, there are many other national parks in Costa Rica waiting to be discovered. From the misty peaks of Chirripó National Park, home to the country's highest mountain, to the volcanic wonders of Tenorio Volcano National Park, with its enchanting blue river, each park offers its own unique blend of wildlife and natural wonders.

Exploring Costa Rica's national parks is an invitation to witness the marvels of the natural world. It is a chance to reconnect with the intricate web of life, to witness the delicate balance between species, and to appreciate the profound beauty that nature bestows upon us. Costa Rica's national parks are a testament to the country's commitment to conservation, and by immersing ourselves in their splendor, we become advocates for their preservation.

So, lace up your hiking boots, grab your binoculars, and embark on a wildlife adventure in Costa Rica's national parks. Let the vibrant colors of birds, the playful antics of monkeys, and the harmony of nature ignite your sense of wonder and appreciation for the incredible biodiversity that thrives within these protected havens. Costa Rica's national parks are truly a wildlife wonderland, inviting you to explore, discover, and revel in the magnificence of the natural world.

Tico Gastronomy: Savoring the Flavors of Costa Rican Cuisine

Welcome to the gastronomic paradise of Costa Rica, where a rich tapestry of flavors and culinary traditions awaits your palate. Tico cuisine, as it is lovingly called, celebrates the country's natural bounty, blending indigenous, Spanish, and Afro-Caribbean influences to create a unique culinary identity that reflects the vibrant spirit of Costa Rica.

At the heart of Costa Rican cuisine is the concept of "sabor casero" or homemade flavor. Traditional dishes are crafted with love and care, using simple yet fresh and locally sourced ingredients that showcase the country's agricultural abundance. From the fertile soils of its valleys to the bounty of its oceans, Costa Rica's culinary heritage is deeply rooted in its natural surroundings.

One of the most iconic dishes of Costa Rican cuisine is gallo pinto, a hearty combination of rice and beans cooked with spices, onion, and sweet pepper. This beloved breakfast staple is often served with scrambled or fried eggs, accompanied by a side of corn tortillas and fresh cheese. Gallo pinto is a true reflection of Tico comfort food, providing a satisfying and nutritious start to the day.

Another staple of Costa Rican cuisine is casado, a well-rounded meal that typically includes rice, beans, a choice of protein (such as chicken, fish, or beef), fried plantains, salad, and often a side of picadillo (a savory mix of diced vegetables). Casado captures the essence of Tico home cooking, offering a balanced combination of flavors and textures that embodies the country's culinary traditions.

Seafood plays a prominent role in Costa Rican cuisine, given the country's extensive coastlines on both the Pacific and Caribbean sides. Ceviche, a refreshing dish of marinated raw fish or shrimp, is a favorite among seafood enthusiasts. The fish or shrimp is marinated in lime juice, mixed with onion, cilantro, and sometimes a hint of fiery chili peppers. This zesty and tangy dish showcases the freshness of the seafood and the vibrant flavors of Costa Rica.

Plantains, a versatile fruit similar to bananas, are a culinary cornerstone in Tico cuisine. They can be prepared in various ways—fried, boiled, or mashed—and are often served as a side dish or incorporated into main courses. Patacones, thick slices of fried plantains, are a popular snack or accompaniment to a meal, while maduros, ripe plantains cooked until caramelized, provide a delightful balance of sweetness to savory dishes.

No exploration of Costa Rican cuisine would be complete without indulging in its vibrant street food culture. On the bustling streets of San José and other cities, you'll find food carts and stalls offering tantalizing treats. Empanadas, filled with cheese, meat, or vegetables and fried to perfection, are a must-try street food delight. Chifrijo, a mouthwatering combination of rice, beans, chicharrones (crispy pork rinds), and pico de gallo, satisfies cravings for a hearty and flavorful snack.

Costa Rica's dedication to sustainable farming and organic practices has led to the rise of farm-to-table experiences and eco-gastronomy. Finca-based restaurants and organic markets offer visitors the opportunity to taste the flavors of the land while supporting local farmers and communities. From farm-fresh vegetables to artisanal cheeses and coffee, these culinary experiences highlight the commitment to quality and sustainability that defines Tico gastronomy.

To quench your thirst, Costa Rica offers a range of refreshing beverages. Chilled coconut water straight from the coconut, locally brewed craft beers, and refrescos naturales, or natural fruit juices, are among the delightful options. Café chorreado, Costa Rican-style drip coffee, is a must for coffee lovers, allowing you to savor the rich aroma and smooth flavors of Costa Rican beans.

Costa Rican cuisine is not just about the flavors—it is also about the warmth and hospitality that accompanies every meal. The concept of "sobremesa," or the time spent lingering at the table after a meal, reflects the Tico culture of conviviality and connection. It's a time to savor the moment, share stories, and cultivate relationships—a true celebration of the joy and togetherness that food brings.

So, embark on a gastronomic adventure through Costa Rica, and let the flavors of Tico cuisine enchant your taste buds. From traditional dishes that evoke a sense of nostalgia to innovative culinary creations that push boundaries, Costa Rican cuisine celebrates the country's cultural heritage and its bountiful natural resources. Savor each bite, embrace the warmth of the Tico culinary tradition, and let the flavors of Costa Rica transport you on a culinary journey like no other.

Mystical Waters: Costa Rica's Healing Hot Springs and Natural Spas

Immerse yourself in the enchanting realm of Costa Rica's healing hot springs and natural spas, where the mystical waters hold the promise of relaxation, rejuvenation, and well-being. Nestled within the country's diverse landscapes, these soothing havens offer a respite from the outside world and invite you to experience the transformative power of nature's healing touch.

Costa Rica is a land blessed with an abundance of volcanic activity, and it is this geothermal energy that gives birth to the country's therapeutic hot springs. The volcanic forces that shape the land also heat the underground water, creating natural pools of warm and mineral-rich waters that have been cherished for their healing properties for centuries.

One of the most renowned destinations for hot springs is the Arenal Volcano region. Here, in the shadow of the majestic volcano, you'll find a multitude of hot springs resorts that cater to every desire for relaxation and indulgence. Picture yourself luxuriating in cascading pools of warm water, surrounded by lush tropical gardens, with a backdrop of verdant rainforests and the volcano's silhouette. The mineral content of these hot springs is believed to have a soothing effect on the body, relieving muscle tension, improving circulation, and promoting overall well-being.

Tabacón, Baldi, and Eco Termales are just a few of the iconic hot springs resorts in the Arenal area. Each offers its own unique ambiance and amenities, but all share a commitment to providing guests with an unforgettable experience of relaxation and healing. Wander through a labyrinth of pools, varying in temperature and size, as you let the warm waters envelop you in their embrace. Unwind under cascading waterfalls, indulge in therapeutic mud treatments, or enjoy a soothing massage to complete your journey of rejuvenation.

Beyond the Arenal region, hot springs can be found throughout the country, each with its own distinct character and setting. In the Guanacaste province, the Rincón de la Vieja area is home to a number of natural hot springs that emerge from the ground, surrounded by the beauty of the national park. These hidden gems offer a more rustic and secluded experience, where you can immerse yourself in the soothing waters amidst the sights and sounds of the forest.

Orosí, located in the Cartago province, is another destination known for its hot springs. Here, you can relax in the thermal pools while gazing out at stunning views of the Orosí Valley and its picturesque surroundings. The serenity and tranquility of this area create a perfect setting for rest and rejuvenation.

Costa Rica's natural spas provide another avenue for wellness and relaxation. From open-air massages to volcanic mud wraps, these spas combine nature's elements with expert treatments to create a truly holistic experience. The lush rainforest settings, the sounds of chirping birds, and the aroma of tropical flowers all contribute to a sense of serenity and balance.

The healing properties of Costa Rica's hot springs and natural spas are not just attributed to the warm waters and therapeutic treatments, but also to the profound connection between nature and well-being. The country's commitment to environmental conservation ensures that these sanctuaries remain unspoiled, allowing visitors to bask in the healing powers of untouched natural beauty.

As you soak in the mystical waters, let go of stress and tension, and embrace the tranquility that surrounds you. Feel the warmth seep into your muscles, revitalizing your body and rejuvenating your spirit. Whether you choose to indulge in a private oasis or soak in the untamed beauty of a hidden spring, Costa Rica's hot springs and natural spas invite you to embark on a journey of self-care and renewal.

So, surrender to the allure of Costa Rica's healing waters, and let the mystical power of these natural wonders envelop you in a world of relaxation and well-being. Allow the soothing embrace of the hot springs and the nurturing touch of nature to restore your balance and awaken your senses. In Costa Rica's hot springs and natural spas, you'll discover a truly transformative experience that celebrates the harmony between body, mind, and the enchanting forces of the natural world.

Sustainable Living: Costa Rica's Commitment to Eco-Tourism

Costa Rica stands as a shining example of sustainable living and a global leader in eco-tourism. With its lush rainforests, diverse ecosystems, and rich biodiversity, the country has embraced a holistic approach to tourism that prioritizes environmental conservation, community engagement, and the well-being of its people. Costa Rica's unwavering commitment to eco-tourism has garnered international recognition and serves as an inspiration for sustainable practices worldwide.

At the heart of Costa Rica's eco-tourism model is the concept of conservation. The country has set aside an impressive 25% of its land as protected areas, national parks, and reserves, ensuring the preservation of its natural treasures. From the enchanting cloud forests of Monteverde to the pristine beaches of Manuel Antonio, these protected areas provide a sanctuary for countless species and offer visitors the opportunity to experience the wonders of nature in a sustainable and responsible manner.

Costa Rica's dedication to sustainability is evident in its renewable energy initiatives. The country is on a path to becoming carbon-neutral by 2021, relying primarily on renewable sources such as hydropower, wind energy, and geothermal energy to meet its electricity needs. This commitment to clean energy has significantly reduced carbon emissions and serves as a testament to Costa Rica's determination to protect its natural resources for future generations.

In line with its sustainable practices, Costa Rica places a strong emphasis on responsible tourism. The country encourages travelers to engage in low-impact activities that respect the environment and local communities. Eco-lodges, ecolodges, and sustainable hotels are dotted throughout the country, offering accommodations that blend seamlessly with nature, utilize renewable resources, and support local communities. These establishments often implement practices such as water and energy conservation, waste management, and organic farming, further reducing their environmental footprint.

Community involvement and empowerment are fundamental components of Costa Rica's eco-tourism model. The country prioritizes the participation of local communities in decision-making processes and ensures that they benefit directly from tourism activities. This approach helps to foster a sense of ownership and pride among communities, encouraging them to protect and preserve their natural and cultural heritage. Community-based tourism initiatives provide opportunities for visitors to engage with locals, learn about their customs, and contribute to the local economy in a sustainable way.

Education and awareness play vital roles in Costa Rica's eco-tourism efforts. The country has implemented programs that promote environmental education, both for locals and visitors. Schools incorporate sustainability into their curricula, raising a generation of environmentally conscious individuals who understand the importance of protecting their natural surroundings. Tour operators and guides play a crucial role in educating visitors about Costa Rica's ecological diversity, encouraging responsible behavior, and highlighting the significance of conservation efforts.

Costa Rica's commitment to eco-tourism extends beyond its borders. The country actively participates in global discussions on sustainable development and hosts international conferences and events focused on environmental issues. Through partnerships with organizations and countries around the world, Costa Rica shares its knowledge and experiences, inspiring others to embrace sustainable practices and contribute to the preservation of our planet. Visiting Costa Rica as an eco-conscious traveler offers a unique opportunity to witness the remarkable achievements and ongoing efforts in sustainable living. From hiking through pristine rainforests and engaging in wildlife conservation projects to supporting local communities and savoring organic and locally sourced cuisine, every aspect of your journey can align with Costa Rica's commitment to eco-tourism.

As you explore this ecological paradise, let the beauty of Costa Rica's landscapes and the warmth of its people inspire you to embrace sustainable living in your own life. Costa Rica's unwavering dedication to eco-tourism serves as a beacon of hope and a reminder that through responsible practices, we can create a harmonious balance between humanity and the natural world. So, embark on a sustainable adventure in Costa Rica, and let the country's commitment to eco-tourism ignite your passion for a more sustainable future. Together, we can follow in the footsteps of Costa Rica and celebrate the interconnectedness of nature, culture, and the well-being of all.

Pacific Paradise: Delving into the Nicoya Peninsula

Welcome to the idyllic Nicoya Peninsula, a Pacific paradise that beckons with its pristine beaches, vibrant wildlife, and a laid-back atmosphere that encapsulates the essence of Costa Rica's pura vida lifestyle. This enchanting region, known for its natural beauty and rich cultural heritage, offers a treasure trove of experiences that will captivate your senses and leave you longing for more.

The Nicoya Peninsula, located on Costa Rica's western coast, is a haven for beach lovers and nature enthusiasts. Its coastline stretches for miles, unveiling an array of breathtaking beaches that cater to all tastes. From the renowned surf breaks of Santa Teresa and Mal País to the secluded coves of Montezuma and the tranquil shores of Samara, there is a beach to suit every mood and preference.

As you dip your toes into the warm Pacific waters, you'll be greeted by an abundance of marine life. Snorkeling and diving opportunities abound, allowing you to explore vibrant coral reefs teeming with tropical fish, graceful sea turtles gliding through the currents, and even the possibility of encountering majestic humpback whales during their annual migration. The marine biodiversity of the Nicoya Peninsula is a testament to Costa Rica's commitment to preserving its coastal ecosystems.

Venturing beyond the shoreline, the Nicoya Peninsula reveals its lush interior, characterized by rolling hills, verdant forests, and picturesque villages. Nature reserves such as Cabo Blanco and Curú showcase the region's ecological diversity, offering hiking trails that wind through dense forests and lead to panoramic viewpoints overlooking the sparkling ocean. Keep your eyes peeled for howler monkeys swinging through the trees, vibrant bird species fluttering by, and elusive coatimundis scurrying along the forest floor.

The Nicoya Peninsula is also known for its longevity. The region is one of the world's designated Blue Zones, areas where people live significantly longer and healthier lives. The traditional lifestyle, rich in physical activity, close-knit communities, and a diet that emphasizes fresh fruits, vegetables, and fish, contributes to the well-being of the local population. As you explore the peninsula, take a moment to appreciate the wisdom and vitality of its residents, who serve as a testament to the power of a balanced and sustainable lifestyle.

The cultural heritage of the Nicoya Peninsula is deeply rooted in its indigenous traditions. The Chorotega people, one of Costa Rica's indigenous groups, have a strong presence in the region. Their handicrafts, pottery, and vibrant artwork showcase their rich cultural heritage and provide visitors with an opportunity to learn about their customs and ancestral wisdom. Local festivals and celebrations offer a glimpse into their vibrant traditions, where traditional dances, music, and costumes bring the spirit of the Chorotega culture to life.

Indulge your taste buds in the flavors of the Nicoya Peninsula, where fresh seafood, tropical fruits, and traditional dishes tantalize your senses. Sample ceviche made with the catch of the day, savor the sweetness of a ripe mango picked from a nearby orchard, or delight in the flavors of a traditional corn tortilla prepared by local artisans. The culinary traditions of the Nicoya Peninsula showcase the region's agricultural bounty and the simplicity of ingredients that make Costa Rican cuisine so delightful.

The Nicoya Peninsula offers a range of accommodation options that cater to different preferences and budgets. From eco-lodges nestled in the heart of nature to luxurious beachfront resorts, the peninsula has something for everyone. Wake up to the sound of crashing waves, take a morning yoga class overlooking the ocean, or simply relax in a hammock as you soak in the laid-back vibes of this Pacific paradise.

Whether you seek adventure, relaxation, or a cultural immersion, the Nicoya Peninsula offers a little slice of paradise that will capture your heart. Embrace the pura vida spirit as you explore its pristine beaches, lush forests, and charming communities. The magic of the Nicoya Peninsula lies in its ability to transport you to a world of natural beauty, tranquility, and the essence of Costa Rica's captivating spirit.

So, venture into the Pacific paradise of the Nicoya Peninsula, and let its beauty and warmth envelop you in a sense of wonder and contentment. Allow the rhythm of the waves, the embrace of the sun, and the welcoming smiles of its people to create lasting memories and a longing to return to this extraordinary corner of Costa Rica.

Carara National Park: Home to Scarlet Macaws and Exquisite Wildlife

Welcome to Carara National Park, a tropical wonderland nestled between the Pacific coast and the lush forests of Costa Rica. This biodiverse paradise offers a glimpse into the captivating world of Scarlet Macaws and an array of exquisite wildlife that calls this pristine ecosystem home. Get ready to embark on a journey of discovery as we explore the wonders of Carara National Park.

Carara National Park is located in the Central Pacific Conservation Area, making it easily accessible from popular tourist destinations like San José, Jacó, and Manuel Antonio. The park spans over 5,000 hectares, encompassing a variety of habitats, including dense rainforests, mangrove swamps, and the Tarcoles River, which borders its northern edge.

The park's rich biodiversity is a testament to its importance as a protected area. Carara is renowned for being one of the best places in Costa Rica to observe the majestic Scarlet Macaw, an iconic and vibrantly colored bird. These magnificent creatures, with their fiery plumage and raucous calls, grace the skies and treetops of Carara, creating a breathtaking spectacle for visitors.

But the Scarlet Macaw is just one of many avian delights that call Carara home. Over 400 species of birds have been recorded in the park, making it a true paradise for birdwatchers. From colorful toucans and trogons to elusive antbirds and hummingbirds, the avian diversity is a testament to the park's healthy ecosystems and abundant food sources.

Carara National Park is also a sanctuary for other wildlife species, both large and small. Keep your eyes peeled for monkeys swinging through the trees, such as the Mantled Howler Monkey and the White-headed Capuchin. Sloths, both the two-toed and three-toed varieties, slowly navigate the forest canopy, blending seamlessly with the foliage. Coatis, raccoons, and agoutis scurry along the forest floor, while colorful poison dart frogs hide among the leaf litter.

The park's diverse habitats provide a haven for reptiles and amphibians as well. Look out for the spectacled caiman sunning themselves along the riverbanks or iguanas basking in the sun. An impressive variety of frogs, including the iconic red-eyed tree frog, showcase their vibrant colors amidst the lush vegetation. The park's natural beauty extends below the surface, where the Tarcoles River and its mangrove estuary support a rich aquatic ecosystem teeming with fish, crustaceans, and reptiles.

Carara National Park offers an extensive network of trails, allowing visitors to explore its natural wonders on foot. The park's knowledgeable guides provide insights into the flora and fauna, sharing their expertise and helping visitors spot hidden gems along the way. The trails wind through towering trees, where orchids and bromeliads cling to branches, creating a magical atmosphere that envelops you in the sights and sounds of the rainforest.

One of the highlights of Carara is the famous Tarcoles River Bridge. This bridge has become an iconic spot for witnessing the impressive congregation of crocodiles in the river below. From the safety of the bridge, you can marvel at the sheer size and power of these ancient reptiles as they sunbathe or glide through the water. It's an awe-inspiring sight that leaves a lasting impression.

Carara National Park's commitment to conservation and sustainability is evident in its efforts to protect and preserve this precious ecosystem. The park collaborates with local communities and organizations to engage in reforestation projects, habitat restoration, and environmental education. These initiatives ensure the long-term survival of the park's unique biodiversity and contribute to Costa Rica's overall commitment to environmental stewardship.

Visiting Carara National Park is a journey of discovery, a chance to connect with the beauty and wonders of Costa Rica's natural heritage. As you explore its trails and witness the vibrant wildlife, let the magic of Carara inspire you to embrace a deeper appreciation for the delicate balance of nature and the importance of protecting our planet's diverse ecosystems.

So, venture into the heart of Carara National Park, and let the vibrant hues of the Scarlet Macaws, the melodic calls of tropical birds, and the enchanting wildlife encounters awaken your sense of wonder. Celebrate the magnificence of Carara and the extraordinary biodiversity that thrives within its boundaries—a testament to Costa Rica's commitment to preserving its natural treasures for generations to come.

A Taste of Paradise: Costa Rica's Exquisite Tropical Fruits

Indulge your senses in the luscious flavors of Costa Rica's exquisite tropical fruits, where every bite is a tantalizing journey into paradise. Nestled in the fertile soils and nourished by the tropical sun, these fruits thrive in Costa Rica's bountiful landscapes, offering a symphony of colors, aromas, and tastes that celebrate the country's rich agricultural heritage. Prepare to embark on a mouthwatering adventure as we explore the vibrant world of Costa Rican tropical fruits.

Mangoes, with their succulent flesh and sweet juiciness, are the crown jewels of Costa Rican fruits. The country boasts an impressive variety of mango cultivars, each with its own distinct flavor and texture. From the Haden, a classic mango with its vibrant orange flesh, to the Tommy Atkins, known for its beautiful red blush, Costa Rica's mangoes offer a burst of tropical sweetness that is unmatched. Bite into a ripe mango and let the juice drip down your chin, savoring the taste of pure paradise.

Papayas, with their vibrant orange flesh and buttery consistency, are another tropical delight that graces Costa Rica's fruit baskets. Known for their digestive properties and high vitamin C content, papayas are both refreshing and nutritious. The Maradol and Red Lady papaya varieties are commonly grown in Costa Rica, delivering a perfect balance of sweetness and tanginess that awakens the taste buds. Enjoy a bowl of fresh papaya in the morning, or savor it in a smoothie or fruit salad for a burst of tropical goodness.

Costa Rica's tropical fruit basket also includes the exotic and enticing pineapple. Known for its juicy sweetness and vibrant golden hue, the country's pineapples are renowned for their exceptional flavor. Costa Rica is one of the largest exporters of pineapples in the world, thanks to its ideal climate and fertile soils. Sink your teeth into a slice of Costa Rican pineapple, and experience the perfect harmony of tangy acidity and tropical sweetness that will transport you to a tropical paradise.

Bananas, a staple in Costa Rican cuisine, are not to be overlooked. The country's banana plantations produce an abundance of this versatile fruit, with the sweet and creamy Cavendish variety being the most commonly consumed. Whether eaten as a quick and nutritious snack, blended into smoothies, or incorporated into traditional dishes like arroz con pollo (rice with chicken), bananas add a touch of tropical delight to every bite.

Costa Rica's tropical fruit medley extends to lesser-known but equally exquisite varieties. The guava, with its aromatic and tropical fragrance, is a favorite among locals and visitors alike. Its pink flesh, dotted with small seeds, offers a unique combination of sweetness and tartness that is truly delightful. Soursop, or guanábana, surprises with its spiky green skin and creamy white flesh, bursting with a tangy and slightly sweet flavor. The carambola, or star fruit, enchants with its distinctive star shape and a delicate balance of sweetness and acidity.

Costa Rica's commitment to organic and sustainable farming practices ensures that these tropical fruits are cultivated with care and respect for the environment. Small-scale farmers and cooperatives play a vital role in preserving the quality and flavor of these fruits, as well as supporting local communities.

Exploring Costa Rica's vibrant markets and fruit stands is a feast for the senses. As you stroll through the colorful stalls, you'll encounter an array of tropical fruits that reflect the country's agricultural diversity. Allow the aroma of ripe mangoes, the vibrant colors of dragon fruits, and the inviting displays of papayas and melons to entice you into a world of tropical abundance.

One of the joys of Costa Rica's tropical fruits is their versatility in culinary applications. From juices and smoothies to refreshing fruit salads and tantalizing desserts, these fruits lend themselves to a myriad of delicious creations. Indulge in a batido, a local fruit smoothie made with fresh tropical fruits blended with ice and a splash of milk. Taste the traditional postre de tres leches, a decadent dessert soaked in a creamy mixture of three types of milk, topped with slices of ripe banana or fresh mango.

Costa Rica's exquisite tropical fruits not only delight the palate, but they also embody the country's vibrant spirit and connection to its natural surroundings. Each bite is a celebration of the country's agricultural heritage, its commitment to sustainability, and its abundant natural resources.

So, savor the flavors of paradise as you relish in the abundance of Costa Rican tropical fruits. Allow their juicy sweetness, tangy zing, and tropical aromas to transport you to the sun-kissed landscapes of this extraordinary country. Celebrate the lusciousness of Costa Rican fruits, and let their divine flavors be a reminder of the joy and beauty that nature bestows upon us.

Monteverde Cloud Forest: An Enchanted Canopy Experience

Welcome to the mystical realm of the Monteverde Cloud Forest, a place where nature's enchantment unfolds amidst mist-shrouded trees and a chorus of exotic birdsong. Nestled in the Tilarán Mountains of Costa Rica, the Monteverde Cloud Forest Reserve offers a captivating journey into a world teeming with biodiversity, stunning vistas, and an ethereal ambiance that is nothing short of magical. Prepare to embark on an extraordinary adventure as we explore the wonders of the Monteverde Cloud Forest.

The Monteverde Cloud Forest Reserve is renowned worldwide for its unique and diverse ecosystem. The combination of high altitude, abundant rainfall, and the meeting of two climatic zones creates the perfect conditions for the development of a cloud forest. This extraordinary phenomenon gives rise to a lush and verdant forest, perpetually enveloped in mist, with an otherworldly beauty that captivates all who enter.

As you venture into the Monteverde Cloud Forest, you'll find yourself immersed in a tapestry of moss-covered trees, epiphytic plants, and an intricate network of trails that wind through this magical realm. Towering giant trees, draped with ethereal curtains of bromeliads and ferns, create a surreal and captivating atmosphere. This verdant wonderland serves as a sanctuary for countless species of flora and fauna, making it a paradise for nature enthusiasts and researchers alike.

One of the most iconic residents of the Monteverde Cloud Forest is the resplendent quetzal. This elusive and vibrantly colored bird, with its emerald green plumage and long, trailing tail feathers, is considered a symbol of beauty and sacredness in Mesoamerican cultures. Spotting a quetzal perched on a moss-covered branch or catching a glimpse of its iridescent feathers amidst the mist is a rare and awe-inspiring experience that epitomizes the magic of the cloud forest.

The Monteverde Cloud Forest is also home to a multitude of other bird species, making it a paradise for birdwatchers. Over 400 bird species have been recorded in the reserve, including hummingbirds, toucans, and the elusive three-wattled bellbird, known for its distinct call that resonates through the misty forest. The vibrant colors, melodious songs, and graceful flights of these feathered inhabitants create a symphony of avian wonder that reverberates through the canopy.

But the enchantment of the Monteverde Cloud Forest extends beyond its avian residents. The forest floor is teeming with life, with a remarkable diversity of amphibians, reptiles, and mammals. As you walk along the trails, you may encounter tiny jewel-like frogs, camouflaged insects, and even the occasional coati or agouti scurrying through the undergrowth. Howler monkeys, capuchin monkeys, and the elusive sloth inhabit the canopy, their presence a testament to the forest's vitality.

The Monteverde Cloud Forest Reserve not only provides a sanctuary for wildlife but also offers a wealth of educational and research opportunities. The reserve is home to several research stations and educational institutions dedicated to the study and conservation of cloud forest ecosystems. Visitors have the chance to participate in guided tours led by knowledgeable naturalists who share their expertise and offer insights into the intricate web of life that exists within the cloud forest.

Exploring the Monteverde Cloud Forest is an adventure in itself, with a range of activities that allow visitors to immerse themselves in this enchanting world. Canopy tours offer a unique perspective as you glide through the treetops on zip lines, providing exhilarating views of the forest and a chance to observe its inhabitants from a different angle. Sky bridges and suspension bridges offer thrilling vantage points, allowing you to traverse the forest canopy and experience the sensation of walking amidst the clouds.

For those seeking a deeper connection with nature, night hikes offer a truly magical experience. As darkness falls, the cloud forest comes alive with the sounds of nocturnal creatures. Guided by the soft glow of flashlights, you'll have the opportunity to witness a whole new cast of characters emerge, including sleeping birds, active insects, and elusive mammals that venture out under the cover of night.

The Monteverde Cloud Forest Reserve is not only a sanctuary for biodiversity but also a testament to Costa Rica's commitment to environmental conservation. The reserve is managed by the Tropical Science Center, a nonprofit organization dedicated to preserving the cloud forest and promoting sustainable practices. The Costa Rican people's embrace of eco-tourism and their recognition of the value of preserving these natural wonders have made the Monteverde Cloud Forest a beacon of hope for conservation efforts worldwide.

Visiting the Monteverde Cloud Forest is an opportunity to connect with the magic of nature and celebrate the extraordinary biodiversity that graces Costa Rica's landscapes. It is a reminder of the interconnectedness of all living beings and the importance of preserving our natural heritage for future generations.

So, step into the enchantment of the Monteverde Cloud Forest and let its mist-laden trails, captivating wildlife, and ethereal beauty awaken your sense of wonder. Celebrate the magnificence of this unique ecosystem, and let its magic inspire you to embrace a deeper appreciation for the intricate and awe-inspiring wonders of the natural world.

Guanacaste: Sun, Sand, and Serenity on the Golden Coast

Welcome to Guanacaste, a land of endless sunshine, pristine beaches, and a sense of serenity that washes over you as soon as you arrive. Located in the northwestern corner of Costa Rica, Guanacaste is known as the "Golden Coast" for its breathtaking stretches of golden sand that meet the azure waters of the Pacific Ocean. Prepare to immerse yourself in a paradise of sun, relaxation, and the laid-back charm that defines the essence of Costa Rica's pura vida lifestyle.

Guanacaste's climate is characterized by its dry season, which runs from November to April, making it an ideal destination for sun-seeking travelers. The region's long, sunny days and warm temperatures create the perfect conditions for lounging on the beach, engaging in water sports, or simply basking in the golden rays of the sun. It's a place where time seems to slow down, allowing you to fully embrace the beauty of your surroundings.

The coastline of Guanacaste is a treasure trove of stunning beaches, each with its own unique charm. Tamarindo, one of the region's most popular destinations, offers a vibrant blend of surf culture, lively nightlife, and a bustling beachfront lined with restaurants and shops. Playa Flamingo boasts pristine white sands and crystal-clear waters, creating an idyllic setting for relaxation and water activities. Further north, Playa Conchal captivates with its shimmering shoreline composed of millions of tiny crushed seashells, creating a unique and unforgettable beach experience.

For those seeking tranquility and seclusion, Guanacaste is home to hidden gems such as Playa Hermosa and Playa Grande. These secluded stretches of sand offer a sense of serenity, where you can unwind and immerse yourself in the natural beauty of the surroundings. Whether you're looking to catch the perfect wave, explore vibrant underwater ecosystems while snorkeling, or simply soak up the sun, Guanacaste's beaches cater to all tastes and preferences.

Beyond its breathtaking coastline, Guanacaste boasts an array of natural wonders waiting to be explored. The region is home to several national parks and protected areas, including Santa Rosa National Park, Rincon de la Vieja National Park, and Palo Verde National Park. These diverse ecosystems encompass dry forests, volcanic landscapes, and wetlands, providing a sanctuary for a wide variety of flora and fauna.

In Santa Rosa National Park, you can wander through ancient dry forests and discover historical landmarks, such as the famous "La Casona," which played a significant role in Costa Rica's history. Rincon de la Vieja National Park offers the opportunity to hike through volcanic landscapes, soak in natural hot springs, and witness the power of geothermal activity with bubbling mud pots and steaming fumaroles. Palo Verde National Park is a haven for birdwatchers, with its wetlands serving as a vital stopover for migratory birds.

Guanacaste is not just a destination for sun and nature enthusiasts—it also showcases Costa Rica's rich cultural heritage. The region's cowboy traditions and "sabanero" culture are deeply rooted in its history. In the town of Liberia, you can immerse yourself in the vibrant atmosphere of the local market, where artisans display their crafts and farmers sell fresh produce. The annual "Fiestas Civicas" celebrate Guanacaste's cultural pride with lively parades, traditional music, and colorful costumes.

When it comes to culinary delights, Guanacaste offers a delectable fusion of traditional Costa Rican cuisine and international flavors. Sample traditional dishes like "casado," a plate that combines rice, beans, plantains, salad, and a choice of meat or fish. Savor fresh seafood caught by local fishermen, including succulent shrimp, red snapper, and lobster. Wash it all down with a refreshing glass of "agua de sapo," a traditional drink made from sugarcane, ginger, and lemon.

Guanacaste's captivating landscapes and warm hospitality make it a popular destination for outdoor activities and eco-adventures. Embark on a thrilling zip-line tour through the treetops of the tropical forest, offering breathtaking views and an adrenaline rush like no other. Take a horseback ride along the beach at sunset, feeling the gentle breeze as you soak in the colors of the sky and the sound of crashing waves. Go on a scuba diving or snorkeling expedition to explore the vibrant underwater world teeming with marine life.

The region's commitment to sustainable tourism is evident in the numerous eco-lodges and nature reserves that embrace eco-friendly practices and support local communities. These establishments offer a blend of comfort and immersion in nature, providing a true eco-tourism experience that allows you to connect with the environment while minimizing your ecological footprint.

Guanacaste's captivating beauty, vibrant culture, and welcoming spirit are a testament to the wonders that Costa Rica has to offer. As you bask in the warmth of the sun, feel the sand between your toes, and immerse yourself in the tranquility of this tropical paradise, let Guanacaste's golden coast become a cherished memory, forever etched in your heart.

So, embrace the pura vida lifestyle on Guanacaste's golden coast, where the sun, sand, and serenity combine to create an unforgettable experience. Celebrate the natural wonders, the warm hospitality, and the rich cultural heritage that make Guanacaste a true gem of Costa Rica's Pacific coast.

Quetzals and Clouds: The Resplendent Beauty of Savegre Valley

Nestled in the heart of Costa Rica's enchanting highlands, the Savegre Valley unveils a world of natural splendor, where mist-laden clouds embrace lush forests, and the resplendent quetzal reigns as a symbol of ethereal beauty. This hidden gem, located in the Talamanca Mountain Range, offers a sanctuary for both wildlife and those seeking a tranquil escape into Costa Rica's pristine landscapes. Prepare to immerse yourself in the resplendent beauty of the Savegre Valley, where quetzals dance among the clouds and nature's wonders abound.

The Savegre Valley is a haven for birdwatchers and nature enthusiasts, renowned for its population of the elusive and stunning resplendent quetzal. This magnificent bird, with its vibrant emerald-green plumage, crimson breast, and long, trailing tail feathers, is considered one of the most beautiful birds in the world. The Savegre Valley is home to one of the largest populations of quetzals in Costa Rica, making it an ideal destination for witnessing their majestic presence.

The cloud forests of the Savegre Valley create a mystical atmosphere, perpetually blanketed in a soft, ethereal mist. This unique climate supports a diverse array of flora and fauna, making it a paradise for naturalists. The valley is adorned with ancient oak trees, draped with mosses, lichens, and epiphytic plants that create a lush green tapestry. Orchids, bromeliads, and ferns add splashes of color to the forest floor, while wildflowers attract hummingbirds and butterflies in a delightful dance of nature's harmony.

Exploring the trails of the Savegre Valley allows you to immerse yourself in its resplendent beauty. The sounds of rushing rivers and cascading waterfalls accompany your journey as you hike through the verdant forest. Keep your eyes peeled for the diverse array of bird species, including toucans, hummingbirds, and colorful tanagers that flit through the foliage. Mammals such as monkeys, sloths, and coatis also call this valley home, their presence adding an extra layer of enchantment to your wilderness experience.

The Savegre River, which winds its way through the valley, is not only a source of life for the surrounding ecosystem but also offers opportunities for outdoor adventures. Fly fishing enthusiasts can cast their lines into its crystal-clear waters, hoping to catch the prized rainbow trout that thrive in its currents. Rafting and kayaking expeditions allow you to navigate the river's twists and turns, offering thrilling encounters with the valley's dramatic landscapes.

The Savegre Valley is also a hub of sustainable and community-based tourism initiatives. Local communities have embraced eco-tourism, establishing lodges and homestays that offer immersive experiences in the valley's natural wonders. These accommodations provide comfort while maintaining a commitment to environmental conservation, ensuring that the beauty of the Savegre Valley can be enjoyed by future generations.

Photographers and artists find inspiration in the Savegre Valley's resplendent beauty. The interplay of light and shadows, the misty clouds embracing the forest, and the vibrant colors of the flora and fauna create a canvas of visual delight. From capturing the grace of a quetzal in flight to immortalizing the delicate details of a moss-covered tree trunk, the Savegre Valley offers endless opportunities for artistic expression.

Beyond its natural wonders, the Savegre Valley is steeped in local culture and traditions. The communities that inhabit the valley's surrounding villages have a strong connection to the land and a deep-rooted appreciation for their natural heritage. Traditional farming practices, handicrafts, and gastronomy reflect the cultural richness of this region. Engaging with the locals offers a glimpse into their way of life and the warmth of their hospitality.

The Savegre Valley serves as a gentle reminder of the importance of conserving Costa Rica's natural wonders. Efforts are in place to protect the valley's delicate ecosystems and promote sustainable practices. The local community and conservation organizations collaborate to ensure the preservation of the valley's biodiversity, as well as the cultural heritage that is intricately intertwined with its landscapes.

Visiting the Savegre Valley is a journey of reverence and appreciation for the resplendent beauty of Costa Rica's highlands. It is an opportunity to reconnect with nature, to marvel at the exquisite quetzal, and to immerse yourself in a world where clouds and forests converge in perfect harmony. Celebrate the Savegre

Valley's resplendent beauty and let its magic leave an indelible mark on your soul.

So, venture into the Savegre Valley, where quetzals and clouds weave a tapestry of resplendent beauty. Allow the mist-laden forests, the melodies of birdsong, and the serenity of this hidden gem to envelop you in a sense of awe and gratitude for the natural wonders that abound in Costa Rica.

Tortuguero National Park: Witnessing the Miracle of Sea Turtles

Welcome to Tortuguero National Park, a place where nature's miracles unfold under a starlit sky and the ancient rhythms of the sea guide the cycle of life. Located on Costa Rica's northeastern Caribbean coast, Tortuguero is a haven for sea turtles, offering a rare opportunity to witness these majestic creatures as they come ashore to lay their eggs. Prepare to embark on a journey of wonder and awe as we explore the natural marvels of Tortuguero National Park.

Tortuguero National Park is named after the Spanish word "tortuga," meaning turtle, and it is rightly recognized as one of the most important nesting sites for sea turtles in the entire Western Hemisphere. Each year, from March to October, thousands of sea turtles return to the dark volcanic sands of Tortuguero's beaches, driven by an ancient instinct to lay their eggs in the very place where they were born.

The park is home to four main species of sea turtles: the green turtle, the hawksbill turtle, the loggerhead turtle, and the critically endangered leatherback turtle. The leatherback turtle, the largest of all sea turtles, can reach lengths of up to seven feet and weigh over a thousand pounds. Witnessing these massive creatures emerge from the depths of the ocean and laboriously make their way up the beach is a humbling and awe-inspiring experience.

Tortuguero National Park's beaches, with their protected nesting areas, provide an ideal habitat for sea turtles. As dusk falls, the beach comes alive with the sound of waves crashing against the shore and the rhythmic digging of turtles creating their nests. Guided night tours offer the opportunity to witness this ancient ritual firsthand, as female turtles dig their nests, deposit their eggs, and carefully cover them with sand before returning to the sea. The sight of a sea turtle meticulously fulfilling her motherly duties is a testament to the resilience and beauty of these magnificent creatures.

Approximately two months later, a different spectacle takes place as the baby turtles hatch and make their way to the ocean. This perilous journey, guided by the moonlight and the reflection of the sea, is a true test of survival for these tiny hatchlings. It is estimated that only one in a thousand will reach adulthood, highlighting the importance of protecting these vulnerable species.

Beyond its sea turtle inhabitants, Tortuguero National Park is a mosaic of diverse ecosystems, including rainforests, wetlands, and lagoons. Its extensive network of canals earned it the nickname "the Amazon of Costa Rica." Exploring the park's waterways by boat or canoe reveals a world teeming with wildlife. Monkeys swing through the trees, caimans lurk along the riverbanks, and a colorful array of birds, including toucans and herons, grace the skies. The park is also home to jaguars, tapirs, and an abundance of reptiles, amphibians, and insects.

The conservation efforts in Tortuguero National Park are crucial to preserving the delicate balance of its ecosystems and protecting the sea turtles that rely on its beaches. The park's management focuses on sustainable tourism practices and community involvement, empowering local residents to actively participate in conservation initiatives and benefit from the park's natural resources in a responsible manner.

Visiting Tortuguero National Park is more than just witnessing the miracle of sea turtles—it's an opportunity to reconnect with the magnificence of nature and to contribute to the conservation of endangered species. The park offers guided tours led by knowledgeable naturalists who provide valuable insights into the ecology of the area, ensuring that visitors leave with a deeper understanding and appreciation for the delicate web of life that exists in Tortuguero.

So, venture into the realm of Tortuguero National Park, where the miracle of sea turtles unfolds against a backdrop of pristine beaches and abundant biodiversity. Celebrate the awe-inspiring cycle of life, the dedication to conservation, and the profound beauty of Costa Rica's natural heritage. Witnessing the majestic sea turtles in this protected sanctuary will leave an indelible mark on your heart, reminding us all of the importance of preserving our precious natural wonders for generations to come.

From Sloths to Howler Monkeys: The Fascinating World of Costa Rican Wildlife

Step into the mesmerizing world of Costa Rican wildlife, where lush rainforests and diverse ecosystems are home to a captivating array of creatures. From the slow-moving sloths that gracefully inhabit the treetops to the thunderous calls of howler monkeys echoing through the canopy, Costa Rica offers a bounty of wildlife encounters that inspire awe and admiration. Prepare to embark on a journey through this fascinating world of Costa Rican wildlife.

Among the most beloved and iconic residents of Costa Rica's rainforests are the sloths. These endearing creatures have captured the hearts of visitors with their gentle nature and slow-paced lifestyle. With their long limbs and hooked claws, sloths spend most of their lives hanging upside down from tree branches, effortlessly blending in with the surrounding foliage. Their leisurely movements and seemingly perpetual smiles remind us to slow down and appreciate the wonders of the natural world.

The enchanting melodies of howler monkeys resonate through Costa Rica's forests, announcing their presence with powerful calls that can be heard for miles. These charismatic primates are known for their distinctive vocalizations, which serve as territorial declarations and communication among group members. Observing a troop of howler monkeys swinging through the treetops, their long tails trailing behind them, is a testament to the incredible agility and adaptability of these arboreal creatures.

Costa Rica's rainforests are also home to an abundance of colorful and unique bird species. The resplendent quetzal, with its emerald-green plumage and long, trailing tail feathers, is considered a crown jewel of the avian world. Its vibrant beauty has inspired legends and captivated the imaginations of people throughout history. Other notable avian residents include toucans, with their oversized bills and vivid hues, and scarlet macaws, which grace the skies with their vibrant red, blue, and yellow feathers.

As you venture deeper into Costa Rica's natural landscapes, you may encounter a variety of reptiles and amphibians. The country is home to an astonishing number of frog species, many of which display striking colors and patterns as a warning to potential predators. The tiny poison dart frogs, with their brilliant hues, are a testament to nature's ingenuity in both defense and beauty. Costa Rica's reptilian inhabitants include caimans, iguanas, and an array of snakes, including the impressive boa constrictor.

Costa Rica's coastal regions are teeming with marine life, offering opportunities for encounters with dolphins, whales, and sea turtles. The Pacific coast serves as a migratory route for humpback whales, which travel thousands of miles to give birth and raise their young in the warm tropical waters. Dolphins playfully swim alongside boats, their graceful movements a testament to their intelligence and social nature. And of course, the sea turtles, including the critically endangered leatherback turtle, return to Costa

Rica's beaches year after year to lay their eggs, carrying on a timeless cycle of life.

Beyond its charismatic megafauna, Costa Rica's biodiversity extends to a vast array of insects, spiders, and small mammals. Leaf-cutter ants march tirelessly, carrying leaf fragments many times their own size, while butterflies flit through the air, their delicate wings showcasing a kaleidoscope of colors. Coatis, raccoons, and kinkajous scurry through the undergrowth, while agoutis and pacas forage for food in the forest floor.

Costa Rica's commitment to conservation and sustainable practices has created protected areas and national parks that serve as havens for wildlife. These areas provide crucial habitats for countless species, allowing them to thrive and continue to contribute to the intricate web of life. Efforts to protect and preserve these natural habitats are essential to ensuring the survival of Costa Rica's remarkable biodiversity for future generations to appreciate and cherish.

Embarking on a wildlife adventure in Costa Rica offers an opportunity to witness the wonders of the natural world firsthand, fostering a deep appreciation for the delicate balance of ecosystems and the incredible diversity of life. Whether you're strolling through the rainforest, gliding along a river in a boat, or simply pausing to observe the intricacies of a tiny insect, the wildlife encounters in Costa Rica are sure to leave a lasting impression.

So, embrace the fascinating world of Costa Rican wildlife, where sloths leisurely traverse the treetops, howler monkeys serenade the forest, and colorful birds fill the air with their vibrant plumage. Celebrate the rich biodiversity and the extraordinary encounters that await in this tropical paradise. Allow Costa Rica's wildlife to ignite your sense of wonder and inspire a deeper appreciation for the natural treasures that grace our planet.

Manuel Antonio National Park: Where the Rainforest Meets the Sea

Welcome to Manuel Antonio National Park, a captivating blend of lush rainforest, pristine beaches, and abundant biodiversity where nature's treasures unfold at the meeting point of land and sea. Located on Costa Rica's central Pacific coast, Manuel Antonio is a tropical paradise that offers a remarkable array of natural wonders and breathtaking landscapes. Prepare to immerse yourself in the splendor of Manuel Antonio National Park, where the rainforest harmoniously coexists with the sparkling waters of the sea.

Manuel Antonio National Park is a testament to Costa Rica's commitment to preserving its natural heritage. It was established in 1972 and covers an area of approximately 1,700 acres, making it one of the country's smallest national parks. However, what it lacks in size, it more than makes up for in its stunning beauty and rich biodiversity.

The park's rainforest is a lush tapestry of green, teeming with life at every turn. Towering trees, including the iconic "ceiba" and "gavilán," create a dense canopy that provides shade and shelter for a multitude of wildlife species. Ferns, bromeliads, and orchids adorn the forest floor, adding splashes of color and fragrance to the vibrant ecosystem.

As you explore the park's network of trails, you'll encounter an astonishing variety of flora and fauna. Keep an eye out for the white-faced capuchin monkeys that swing gracefully through the trees, their curious eyes watching your every move. Sloths, with their leisurely movements, cling to branches, seemingly unperturbed by the bustling activity around them. Agile iguanas bask in the sun, while vividly colored butterflies flit through the air, creating a kaleidoscope of beauty.

One of the highlights of Manuel Antonio National Park is its pristine beaches. Four stunning beaches—Espadilla Sur, Manuel Antonio, Escondido, and Playita—beckon visitors with their golden sands and crystal-clear waters. These idyllic coastal stretches offer a tranquil escape, where you can bask in the sun, swim in the gentle waves, or simply relax and soak up the natural beauty that surrounds you.

The park's marine environment is just as captivating as its terrestrial wonders. Snorkeling and scuba diving enthusiasts will be delighted by the vibrant underwater world that awaits beneath the surface. Coral reefs teem with colorful fish, and if you're lucky, you may even spot a graceful sea turtle gliding by. Dolphins frolic in the waves, their playful antics a joy to behold.

One of the most iconic features of Manuel Antonio National Park is Punta Catedral, a dramatic rock formation that juts out into the sea, resembling a cathedral spire. The panoramic views from this vantage point are simply breathtaking, offering sweeping vistas of the Pacific Ocean and the lush coastline.

The park's commitment to conservation is evident in its efforts to protect endangered species. Manuel Antonio National Park is home to the endangered squirrel monkeys, which can be seen leaping from tree to tree in agile acrobatic displays. The park also serves as a crucial habitat for the elusive and endangered three-toed sloth, providing a sanctuary for their survival.

To explore Manuel Antonio National Park fully, it is recommended to take advantage of the knowledgeable local guides who can enhance your experience with their expertise and insights. They can point out hidden wildlife, explain the intricate relationships within the ecosystem, and share fascinating stories about the park's natural and cultural history.

Manuel Antonio National Park is a place of wonder and natural harmony, where the beauty of the rainforest meets the serenity of the sea. It is a testament to Costa Rica's commitment to environmental conservation and sustainable tourism practices. The juxtaposition of the diverse ecosystems—from the vibrant rainforest to the pristine beaches—makes Manuel Antonio a truly unique and magical destination.

So, immerse yourself in the splendor of Manuel Antonio National Park, where the rainforest meets the sea in a symphony of natural beauty. Celebrate the rich biodiversity, the breathtaking landscapes, and the sense of tranquility that envelops this coastal paradise. Allow Manuel Antonio to awaken your senses, ignite your spirit of adventure, and leave an indelible imprint of wonder and appreciation for Costa Rica's remarkable natural treasures.

Bridging Past and Present: Costa Rica's Historic Landmarks

Costa Rica's rich history and cultural heritage come alive through its historic landmarks, each one a testament to the country's vibrant past and enduring legacy. From colonial architecture to ancient archaeological sites, Costa Rica's historic landmarks bridge the gap between past and present, offering a glimpse into the diverse tapestry of the nation's identity. Join us as we embark on a journey through time, celebrating the treasures that connect Costa Rica's past with its vibrant present.

1. San José Cathedral: Located in the heart of Costa Rica's capital city, the San José Cathedral is an architectural gem that showcases the country's religious heritage. With its neoclassical façade and intricate stained glass windows, the cathedral is a symbol of faith and a prominent landmark in San José.
2. National Theater of Costa Rica: A true cultural icon, the National Theater of Costa Rica stands as a testament to the country's love for the arts. This majestic theater, adorned with opulent interiors and intricate details, hosts a variety of performances, including ballets, operas, and theater productions. It is a hub of artistic expression and a source of national pride.
3. Guayabo National Monument: Delve into Costa Rica's pre-Columbian history at the Guayabo National Monument, an ancient archaeological site that dates back over 3,000 years. Located near the city of Turrialba, this enigmatic site

features stone structures, petroglyphs, and remnants of an advanced water management system, providing valuable insights into the indigenous civilizations that once thrived in the region.
4. Orosi Church: Nestled in the picturesque Orosi Valley, the Orosi Church is the oldest church still in use in Costa Rica. Built in 1743, this colonial-era church showcases Spanish colonial architecture and serves as a place of worship for the local community. Its historical significance and serene setting make it a must-visit landmark.
5. Fortín de Heredia: Explore the Fortín de Heredia, a military fortress that played a pivotal role in Costa Rica's fight for independence. Located in the city of Heredia, this well-preserved structure offers a glimpse into the country's past struggles and serves as a reminder of the courage and resilience of its people.
6. Guayabo de Turrialba Archaeological Site: Step back in time at the Guayabo de Turrialba Archaeological Site, one of the country's most important archaeological sites. This ancient city was once a thriving center of indigenous civilization, featuring stone streets, plazas, and ceremonial structures. Visitors can wander through the site and imagine the vibrant life that once existed there.
7. Cartago Ruins: Discover the remnants of Cartago, the former capital of Costa Rica. Destroyed by earthquakes in the 18th century, the ruins stand as a testament to the city's historical significance and the resilience of its inhabitants. The Cartago Ruins offer a glimpse

into the country's colonial past and provide a tranquil setting for reflection and contemplation.
8. Guanacaste's Colonial Towns: Explore the colonial towns of Guanacaste, such as Nicoya and Liberia, which are steeped in history and charm. Walking through the narrow cobblestone streets, visitors can admire colonial architecture, visit local museums, and immerse themselves in the cultural heritage of the region.
9. Santa Rosa National Park: The historical significance of Santa Rosa National Park cannot be overstated. It was the site of the Battle of Santa Rosa in 1856, a crucial event in Costa Rica's fight against filibuster William Walker and his forces. Today, visitors can explore the park's historical buildings and monuments while also enjoying its natural beauty and biodiversity.
10. La Aduana Cultural Center: Housed in a beautifully restored historic building in San José, La Aduana Cultural Center serves as a cultural hub, showcasing art exhibitions, concerts, and theatrical performances. It combines the preservation of Costa Rica's architectural heritage with the celebration of contemporary arts and culture.

These are just a few examples of the many historic landmarks that grace Costa Rica's landscape, connecting the past with the present and enriching the country's cultural fabric. Each site tells a story, allowing visitors to delve into the layers of Costa Rica's history and appreciate the enduring influence of the past on the country's vibrant present.

So, embrace the bridging of past and present as you explore Costa Rica's historic landmarks, from awe-inspiring colonial architecture to ancient archaeological sites. Celebrate the nation's rich heritage, the resilience of its people, and the enduring legacies that shape Costa Rica's cultural identity. Let these historic landmarks serve as windows into the country's captivating past and be a source of inspiration for a future filled with pride, appreciation, and a deep connection to Costa Rica's vibrant heritage.

Osa Peninsula: A Pristine Wilderness Teeming with Life

Welcome to the Osa Peninsula, a haven of untamed wilderness that brims with life and captivates the senses. Located on Costa Rica's southern Pacific coast, the Osa Peninsula is a treasure trove of biodiversity and natural wonders. This remote and pristine region is celebrated as one of the most biodiverse places on Earth, where a remarkable variety of habitats converge to create an ecological masterpiece. Join us as we embark on a journey through the Osa Peninsula, celebrating its pristine wilderness and the abundant life it sustains.

1. Corcovado National Park: At the heart of the Osa Peninsula lies Corcovado National Park, a true crown jewel of Costa Rica's protected areas. This untouched paradise encompasses nearly half of the peninsula, making it the largest national park in the country. Corcovado is a sanctuary for an astonishing array of wildlife, including jaguars, tapirs, scarlet macaws, and all four species of Costa Rica's monkeys.
2. Pristine Beaches: The Osa Peninsula boasts some of Costa Rica's most pristine and secluded beaches. From the palm-fringed shores of Carate to the dramatic cliffs of Drake Bay, these coastal gems offer a serene escape into nature's embrace. Whether you're seeking a tranquil spot for relaxation or an opportunity to witness nesting sea turtles, the beaches of the Osa Peninsula deliver unforgettable experiences.

3. Golfo Dulce: The Osa Peninsula is blessed with Golfo Dulce, a gulf teeming with marine life. This unique and biodiverse marine ecosystem provides a sanctuary for dolphins, humpback whales, sea turtles, and an abundance of fish species. Snorkeling, kayaking, and boating in Golfo Dulce offer a chance to immerse yourself in the wonders of the underwater world.
4. Primary Rainforests: The Osa Peninsula is predominantly covered by primary rainforests, representing some of the last remaining intact tropical rainforests in Central America. Towering trees, dense vegetation, and a symphony of bird songs create an immersive experience in nature. The lush foliage harbors countless species of flora and fauna, from towering ceiba trees to delicate orchids and colorful bromeliads.
5. Scarlet Macaws: The Osa Peninsula is famous for its vibrant scarlet macaws, which grace the skies with their brilliant plumage and raucous calls. These magnificent birds find sanctuary in the peninsula's forests, their presence adding a splash of color and excitement to the surrounding wilderness. Witnessing a flock of scarlet macaws in flight is a sight to behold and a reminder of Costa Rica's commitment to conservation.
6. Endangered Species: The Osa Peninsula provides a critical refuge for numerous endangered species. The elusive and endangered Baird's tapir finds solace in the peninsula's protected areas, while the endangered Central American squirrel monkey swings through the trees with agility. The peninsula is also home to

the charismatic and endangered harpy eagle, a majestic raptor that patrols the skies with its piercing gaze.
7. Sirena Ranger Station: Located within Corcovado National Park, the Sirena Ranger Station serves as a base for explorations into the park's wilderness. Here, visitors can embark on guided hikes, encounter wildlife up close, and gain a deeper understanding of the park's ecology through the expertise of local guides. The station offers a unique opportunity to connect with the untamed beauty of the Osa Peninsula.
8. Indigenous Communities: The Osa Peninsula is also home to indigenous communities, including the Bribri and Boruca peoples, who have inhabited the region for centuries. These communities have a deep connection with the land and possess a wealth of traditional knowledge about the forest's resources and medicinal plants. Engaging with these communities offers a glimpse into their rich cultural heritage and their harmonious relationship with nature.
9. Biodiversity Hotspot: The Osa Peninsula is recognized as a biodiversity hotspot, meaning it harbors a high concentration of unique species found nowhere else on Earth. Its geographic location, varied topography, and protected status contribute to its extraordinary richness in biodiversity. Scientists and nature enthusiasts flock to the peninsula to study and marvel at its ecological marvels.

The Osa Peninsula is a sanctuary of unparalleled natural beauty and a testament to Costa Rica's commitment to conservation. Its pristine wilderness and abundant biodiversity provide a sanctuary for countless species, reminding us of the interconnectedness and fragility of our planet's ecosystems.

So, embrace the wonders of the Osa Peninsula, a place where wilderness reigns and life thrives. Celebrate its untouched beauty, the symphony of sounds that echo through its rainforests, and the chance encounters with rare and remarkable creatures. Let the Osa Peninsula ignite a sense of wonder, inspire a deeper appreciation for our natural world, and remind us all of the importance of preserving these precious habitats for generations to come.

Diving into the Deep Blue: Exploring Costa Rica's Underwater Treasures

Dive into the deep blue waters of Costa Rica and immerse yourself in a world of underwater treasures. From vibrant coral reefs to mesmerizing marine life, Costa Rica offers a diving paradise that is sure to captivate both seasoned divers and beginners alike. Prepare to explore the breathtaking underwater landscapes and encounter a stunning array of marine creatures as we embark on a journey to celebrate Costa Rica's underwater wonders.

Costa Rica's Pacific and Caribbean coasts are renowned for their diverse and thriving marine ecosystems. Here, warm waters teem with life, and a kaleidoscope of colors awaits beneath the surface.

1. Cocos Island: Located 550 kilometers off the Pacific coast of Costa Rica, Cocos Island is a UNESCO World Heritage Site and a mecca for diving enthusiasts. Its remote and protected status has allowed its underwater ecosystem to flourish, making it one of the best places in the world for diving with large pelagic species. Divers can encounter massive schools of hammerhead sharks, graceful manta rays, and even the elusive whale shark.
2. Caño Island Biological Reserve: Situated in the waters of the Pacific, near the Osa Peninsula, Caño Island is another prime diving destination. The marine biodiversity surrounding the island is astounding, with clear visibility and an

abundance of marine life. Divers can explore vibrant coral formations, swim alongside sea turtles, and marvel at the colorful inhabitants of the reef, including parrotfish, angelfish, and moray eels.

3. Bat Islands: Located in the Gulf of Papagayo on the Pacific coast, the Bat Islands (Islas Murciélagos) are renowned for their encounters with bull sharks. These magnificent creatures, known for their power and presence, gather in these waters, providing an exhilarating and unique diving experience for those seeking a thrilling adventure beneath the waves.

4. Gandoca-Manzanillo Wildlife Refuge: On Costa Rica's Caribbean coast, the Gandoca-Manzanillo Wildlife Refuge offers divers a chance to explore the lesser-explored underwater wonders. This protected area is home to vibrant coral reefs, seagrass beds, and mangrove forests, providing habitats for an array of marine life, including seahorses, stingrays, and colorful reef fish.

5. Underwater Rock Formations: Costa Rica's underwater landscapes are not limited to coral reefs. Along its coasts, divers can also explore unique rock formations that serve as underwater habitats. The underwater pinnacles of the Catalina Islands, for example, offer a playground for divers to encounter reef sharks, eagle rays, and an abundance of tropical fish. The dramatic rock formations provide intriguing nooks and crannies for marine life to hide and thrive.

6. Macro Diving: Beyond the larger marine creatures, Costa Rica's waters are a haven for

macro enthusiasts. Underwater photographers and divers with a keen eye can discover a world of tiny and fascinating marine organisms. From nudibranchs in vibrant hues to camouflaged seahorses, the intricate details of these underwater wonders are a testament to the diversity of life in Costa Rica's seas.

Costa Rica's commitment to marine conservation and sustainable tourism practices ensures the preservation of its underwater treasures. Dive operators and organizations work hand in hand to protect the fragile marine ecosystems, educate divers about responsible diving practices, and contribute to scientific research.

So, take the plunge and discover the wonders of Costa Rica's underwater realm. Celebrate the vibrancy of its coral reefs, the grace of its marine giants, and the hidden gems that await beneath the waves. Let the magic of diving in Costa Rica ignite a sense of wonder, inspire a deeper connection to the ocean, and foster a commitment to protect these precious underwater treasures for generations to come.

Celestial Delights: Stargazing in Costa Rica's Dark Skies

Look up to the heavens and behold the celestial wonders that adorn Costa Rica's dark skies. Far away from the bright lights of urban areas, Costa Rica offers stargazers a rare opportunity to immerse themselves in a celestial symphony of stars, planets, and cosmic phenomena. With its pristine natural landscapes and protected areas, Costa Rica provides the perfect backdrop for an enchanting journey into the cosmos. Let us celebrate the celestial delights and the awe-inspiring beauty of stargazing in Costa Rica.

1. Dark Sky Reserves: Costa Rica is committed to preserving its dark skies and has established Dark Sky Reserves to protect its pristine nocturnal environments. These reserves, such as the Central Valley Dark Sky Reserve and the Osa Peninsula Dark Sky Reserve, provide optimal conditions for stargazing, ensuring minimal light pollution and maximum visibility of the night sky.
2. Abundance of Stars: In Costa Rica's dark skies, a breathtaking expanse of stars reveals itself. On a clear night, away from the city lights, the Milky Way stretches across the firmament, casting its ethereal glow. Countless stars twinkle above, forming constellations that have inspired human imagination for centuries.
3. Shooting Stars and Meteor Showers: Costa Rica offers the opportunity to witness spectacular shooting stars and meteor showers. During peak meteor shower events, such as the Perseids or

the Geminids, shooting stars streak across the sky in mesmerizing displays. Find a comfortable spot, lay back, and let the celestial fireworks unfold.

4. Planetary Marvels: The dark skies of Costa Rica allow for excellent views of our neighboring planets. With a telescope or even with the naked eye, you can observe the gas giants Jupiter and Saturn, their majestic rings and Galilean moons captivating stargazers of all ages. Mars, with its rusty red hue, occasionally comes close enough to reveal its surface features.

5. Cosmic Events and Eclipses: Costa Rica has been fortunate to witness rare celestial events. In recent years, it became a prime location for observing total solar eclipses. The thrilling experience of witnessing the moon completely obscure the sun and the world plunging into temporary darkness is an unforgettable memory etched in the hearts of those fortunate enough to witness it.

6. Wildlife by Night: Stargazing in Costa Rica goes beyond the celestial wonders. As night falls, the wildlife awakens, adding a touch of magic to the experience. Listen to the chorus of nocturnal creatures, such as howler monkeys and tree frogs, serenading the night. Fireflies dance among the trees, and the sparkling bioluminescence of marine organisms illuminates the coastal waters.

7. Stargazing Tours and Observatories: Costa Rica offers guided stargazing tours and access to observatories equipped with telescopes. Knowledgeable guides provide insight into the cosmos, sharing astronomical knowledge and

pointing out celestial objects of interest. These experiences deepen the appreciation for the wonders of the universe and leave a lasting impression.
8. Harmony with Nature: Stargazing in Costa Rica is not only a journey into the cosmos but also a reminder of the country's commitment to preserving its natural environment. The protection of dark skies goes hand in hand with the conservation of natural habitats, promoting harmony between humanity and nature.

As you gaze up at the celestial dome in Costa Rica, allow yourself to be captivated by the immensity of the universe and the beauty of the night sky. Celebrate the wonder and interconnectedness of it all, fostering a sense of awe and appreciation for the vastness of the cosmos and the preciousness of our planet.

So, embrace the celestial delights that await in Costa Rica's dark skies. Celebrate the countless stars, the dancing meteors, and the mysteries of the universe that unfold overhead. Let the beauty of the night sky inspire a sense of wonder, ignite a curiosity for the cosmos, and remind us of the immense beauty that lies beyond our earthly boundaries.

Nicoya: Secrets of Longevity and Happiness

Discover the secrets of longevity and happiness in the enchanting region of Nicoya, Costa Rica. Nestled on the Nicoya Peninsula, this captivating corner of the country has gained worldwide recognition for its high concentration of centenarians and the remarkable well-being enjoyed by its residents. Join us as we delve into the unique factors that contribute to the longevity and happiness of Nicoya's inhabitants, celebrating the essence of this extraordinary place.

1. Blue Zones: Nicoya is one of the few regions on Earth designated as a Blue Zone—an area where people live longer and healthier lives. This distinction has drawn the attention of scientists and researchers eager to uncover the secrets behind the exceptional longevity observed in Nicoya.
2. Active Lifestyle: The residents of Nicoya maintain an active lifestyle, engaging in daily physical activities that contribute to their overall well-being. Whether it's tending to their crops, walking long distances, or participating in traditional dances, physical movement is an integral part of their daily routine.
3. Nutritious Diet: The traditional diet of Nicoyans is centered around fresh, locally sourced ingredients. Abundant in fruits, vegetables, legumes, and whole grains, their diet is rich in nutrients and low in processed foods. This plant-based diet, combined with a moderate

consumption of lean proteins, contributes to their overall health and longevity.
4. Clean Air and Natural Environment: Nicoya's pristine natural environment provides clean air and abundant green spaces, creating an ideal setting for a healthy and balanced lifestyle. The lush landscapes, unpolluted air, and proximity to nature nurture the physical and mental well-being of its residents.
5. Strong Community Bonds: Nicoya is renowned for its tight-knit communities, where strong social connections and a sense of belonging are deeply ingrained. These social ties create a support system that fosters emotional well-being, reduces stress, and promotes a positive outlook on life.
6. Positive Attitude: The people of Nicoya embody a positive and optimistic outlook on life. Their mindset, characterized by resilience, gratitude, and a strong sense of purpose, contributes to their overall happiness and well-being. They embrace life's challenges with grace and find joy in the simple pleasures of everyday living.
7. Cultural Heritage: Nicoya is steeped in rich cultural heritage, and its residents hold onto age-old traditions that promote well-being and a strong sense of identity. From traditional ceremonies and festivals to the passing down of ancestral wisdom, the preservation of cultural practices nurtures a deep-rooted sense of purpose and connection to the past.
8. Natural Remedies and Healing Practices: Nicoya has a long history of traditional healing practices and herbal remedies. The use of medicinal plants and natural therapies, passed

down through generations, contributes to the overall health and vitality of its residents.
9. Low Stress Levels: The relaxed pace of life in Nicoya, away from the hustle and bustle of urban centers, contributes to lower stress levels. The peacefulness and tranquility of the region allow its inhabitants to enjoy a slower, more balanced lifestyle that promotes overall well-being.
10. Proximity to Nature: Nicoya's proximity to breathtaking natural wonders, such as pristine beaches, lush forests, and stunning waterfalls, provides ample opportunities for residents to engage in outdoor activities and connect with nature. This connection to the natural world nurtures a sense of serenity, harmony, and rejuvenation.

The secrets of longevity and happiness found in Nicoya are a testament to the remarkable lifestyle and environment that this region offers. It serves as an inspiration for cultivating a life filled with vitality, purpose, and contentment.

So, immerse yourself in the wonders of Nicoya, where longevity and happiness intertwine. Celebrate the vibrant culture, embrace the active lifestyle, and savor the bountiful natural beauty that surrounds this remarkable region. Let Nicoya inspire you to live a life of balance, joy, and well-being, as you uncover the secrets of longevity and happiness that have made this corner of Costa Rica so extraordinary.

Hidden Gems: Costa Rica's Off-the-Beaten-Path Destinations

Beyond the well-known attractions lie Costa Rica's hidden gems, off-the-beaten-path destinations that offer a glimpse into untouched natural beauty, cultural heritage, and unforgettable experiences. These hidden treasures, tucked away in lesser-explored corners of the country, unveil a different side of Costa Rica—a side that celebrates tranquility, adventure, and authentic encounters. Join us as we embark on a journey to discover the hidden gems of Costa Rica, celebrating their unique charm and the joy of exploration.

1. Drake Bay: Located on the northern tip of the Osa Peninsula, Drake Bay is a secluded coastal paradise that captivates visitors with its pristine beaches, lush rainforests, and abundant wildlife. This hidden gem offers opportunities for snorkeling, kayaking, and hiking, allowing travelers to immerse themselves in nature's embrace.
2. Rio Celeste: Nestled within Tenorio Volcano National Park, Rio Celeste is a natural wonder that enchants all who venture there. Its ethereal turquoise waters, formed by a unique chemical reaction, create a breathtaking sight. Exploring the park's trails leads to hidden waterfalls, hot springs, and lush vegetation, rewarding intrepid travelers with a magical experience.
3. Tortuguero: Known as Costa Rica's "Little Amazon," Tortuguero National Park is a hidden gem accessible only by boat or plane. This pristine wilderness is a haven for wildlife

enthusiasts, offering a chance to encounter nesting sea turtles, monkeys, colorful birds, and caimans as you navigate through the park's intricate network of canals.
4. Playa Conchal: Tucked away on the Pacific coast, Playa Conchal is a beach paradise renowned for its unique sands composed of tiny crushed seashells. This hidden gem offers a tranquil retreat where visitors can relax on pristine shores, snorkel in crystal-clear waters, and witness stunning sunsets.
5. Cahuita: On Costa Rica's Caribbean coast lies the charming town of Cahuita, a hidden gem known for its relaxed atmosphere, Afro-Caribbean culture, and Cahuita National Park. The park protects vibrant coral reefs, allowing snorkelers to witness an underwater world teeming with colorful fish, rays, and even the occasional sea turtle.
6. Chirripó National Park: For those seeking a true mountain adventure, Chirripó National Park awaits. This hidden gem is home to Cerro Chirripó, Costa Rica's highest peak. Hiking to its summit rewards intrepid trekkers with breathtaking vistas, encompassing both the Pacific and Caribbean coasts on a clear day.
7. Rio Savegre: In the heart of the Talamanca Mountains lies the Rio Savegre, a hidden gem for nature lovers and adventure seekers. This pristine river is ideal for whitewater rafting, kayaking, and birdwatching, offering a thrilling yet serene escape into Costa Rica's unspoiled wilderness.
8. San Gerardo de Dota: Tucked away in the mountains of the Los Santos region, San

Gerardo de Dota is a hidden gem for birdwatching enthusiasts and nature lovers. Its cloud forests provide a habitat for the resplendent quetzal, one of the most sought-after bird species in Costa Rica.

9. Nosara: Situated on the Nicoya Peninsula, Nosara is a hidden gem that combines pristine beaches, lush forests, and a laid-back surf culture. This off-the-beaten-path destination offers an ideal setting for yoga retreats, wellness getaways, and reconnecting with nature.
10. Turrialba: Nestled in the Central Valley, Turrialba is a hidden gem known for its stunning landscapes, rural charm, and proximity to the active Turrialba Volcano. Outdoor enthusiasts can explore the region's rivers, waterfalls, and coffee plantations while enjoying the warmth and hospitality of the local community.

These hidden gems of Costa Rica beckon the adventurous at heart, offering authentic experiences, unspoiled natural beauty, and a chance to connect with the country's rich cultural and ecological heritage.

So, venture off the beaten path and embrace the allure of Costa Rica's hidden gems. Celebrate the joy of discovery, the thrill of exploration, and the satisfaction of uncovering the secrets that lie beyond the tourist trails. Let these hidden treasures ignite your sense of adventure, and may they leave an indelible mark on your heart as you create cherished memories in the lesser-explored corners of this remarkable country.

Arenal Volcano: Adventure and Relaxation in the Shadow of Fire

Nestled in the heart of Costa Rica, the Arenal Volcano stands as an iconic symbol of the country's natural beauty and geological prowess. Majestic and awe-inspiring, this active volcano beckons adventurers and relaxation seekers alike to bask in its volcanic wonders. Join us as we explore the captivating allure of Arenal Volcano, celebrating the perfect blend of adventure and relaxation that awaits in the shadow of fire.

1. Volcanic Majesty: Arenal Volcano, with its perfectly conical shape, rises dramatically from the surrounding lush landscapes. Its imposing presence commands attention, drawing visitors from around the world to witness its raw power and dynamic beauty.
2. Active Volcano: Arenal Volcano has been one of the most active volcanoes in Costa Rica, with frequent eruptions and volcanic activity in the past. While it entered a resting phase in 2010, its legacy as a dynamic and awe-inspiring force of nature continues to captivate the imagination of those who visit.
3. Volcanic Hot Springs: Arenal's volcanic activity has blessed the region with a network of hot springs, where visitors can soak in mineral-rich thermal waters surrounded by lush tropical landscapes. These rejuvenating thermal springs offer a relaxing and therapeutic experience, soothing both the body and the soul.
4. Adventure Activities: Arenal Volcano is a playground for adventure enthusiasts, offering a

wide array of thrilling activities. Hike through the volcano's trails, traversing its lava fields and exploring the remnants of past eruptions. Zipline through the treetops, taking in breathtaking views of the volcano and surrounding rainforest. Embark on a whitewater rafting adventure down the nearby rivers, feeling the rush of adrenaline as you navigate the rapids.

5. Arenal Lake: Located at the base of the volcano, Arenal Lake is a shimmering gem that adds to the region's allure. The largest lake in Costa Rica, it offers opportunities for boating, kayaking, and fishing, with the majestic volcano providing a stunning backdrop to your aquatic adventures.

6. Wildlife and Biodiversity: The Arenal Volcano area is teeming with biodiversity, offering nature lovers the chance to spot a wide variety of flora and fauna. From colorful toucans and elusive sloths to vibrant orchids and towering ceiba trees, the region showcases Costa Rica's remarkable natural heritage.

7. Arenal Observatory: The Arenal Observatory Lodge provides a unique vantage point for experiencing the volcano's grandeur. Located on the outskirts of Arenal Volcano National Park, this lodge offers stunning panoramic views and educational opportunities. Explore the hiking trails, visit the observatory deck, and learn about the volcano's history and its impact on the surrounding ecosystem.

8. Lush Rainforests: The Arenal Volcano region is enveloped in lush rainforests that are home to an incredible array of plant and animal species.

Explore the trails that wind through the dense foliage, listening to the symphony of bird calls and the rustling of leaves. It's a chance to connect with nature on a profound level and appreciate the biodiversity that thrives in Costa Rica's protected areas.
9. Cultural Experiences: In addition to its natural wonders, the Arenal Volcano region offers opportunities to immerse oneself in Costa Rica's vibrant culture. Visit the nearby town of La Fortuna, where you can sample traditional cuisine, browse local markets for handicrafts, and interact with friendly locals who embody the warmth and hospitality for which Costa Rica is known.
10. Tranquility and Relaxation: Amidst the excitement of adventure, the Arenal Volcano area also offers tranquility and relaxation. Unwind in eco-lodges and boutique resorts that blend seamlessly with the surrounding nature. Wake up to the symphony of birdsong, practice yoga in serene settings, or indulge in spa treatments that incorporate natural volcanic elements—allowing the volcano's energy to infuse a sense of peace and well-being.

Arenal Volcano embodies the remarkable spirit of Costa Rica, where adventure and relaxation coexist harmoniously. It invites visitors to embrace their sense of exploration, indulge in thrilling activities, and find solace in the serene beauty of the natural world.

So, venture into the shadow of fire, where adventure and relaxation converge in the presence of Arenal Volcano. Celebrate its majestic beauty, soak in rejuvenating hot springs, and create lasting memories amidst this iconic symbol of Costa Rica's volcanic heritage. Let the allure of Arenal Volcano ignite your spirit of adventure and inspire moments of tranquility and reflection as you immerse yourself in this captivating corner of the country.

The Blue Zone of Costa Rica: A Fountain of Youth in the Nicoya Peninsula

In the remote reaches of the Nicoya Peninsula in Costa Rica lies a remarkable place that has captured the attention of researchers and health enthusiasts worldwide—the Blue Zone of Costa Rica. Known for its high concentration of centenarians and exceptional longevity, this region offers a fascinating insight into the secrets of a long and vibrant life. Join us as we explore the Blue Zone of Costa Rica, celebrating its status as a veritable fountain of youth and a testament to the country's commitment to well-being.

1. Longevity at its Best: The Nicoya Peninsula has gained recognition as one of the world's five Blue Zones—a term coined by author Dan Buettner to describe regions where people live longer, healthier lives. The Blue Zone of Costa Rica boasts an impressive number of centenarians, with residents experiencing remarkable longevity and vitality.
2. Lifestyle Factors: The longevity observed in the Blue Zone of Costa Rica can be attributed to a combination of lifestyle factors that contribute to overall well-being. These factors include a nutritious diet, active lifestyle, strong social connections, and a sense of purpose and belonging.
3. Nutritious Diet: The diet of Nicoyans, the inhabitants of the Blue Zone, is based on simple, whole foods. Fresh fruits and vegetables, beans, corn, and locally sourced ingredients form the

foundation of their diet. This plant-centric approach, along with moderate portions of lean proteins, contributes to their overall health and vitality.
4. Centenarian Populations: The Nicoya Peninsula boasts a significantly higher concentration of centenarians compared to other regions around the world. The prevalence of individuals reaching the age of 100 and beyond is a testament to the positive impact of lifestyle and environmental factors on longevity.
5. Physical Activity: The active lifestyle of Nicoyans plays a pivotal role in their longevity. Daily physical activities, such as tending to crops, walking long distances, and engaging in traditional dances, keep the body in motion and promote overall well-being.
6. Social Connections: The strong social bonds and sense of community in the Blue Zone of Costa Rica contribute to the well-being and longevity of its residents. The tight-knit communities foster a support system that promotes emotional health, reduces stress, and enhances overall quality of life.
7. Sense of Purpose: Nicoyans maintain a strong sense of purpose and belonging, even in their advanced years. The intergenerational connections, respect for elders, and active participation in community life contribute to their continued engagement and satisfaction with life.
8. Natural Environment: The Nicoya Peninsula's natural environment plays a crucial role in the well-being of its inhabitants. The clean air, abundant green spaces, and proximity to nature

create a harmonious setting that promotes physical and mental health.
9. Positive Outlook: The residents of the Blue Zone exhibit a positive attitude towards life, embracing a mindset of gratitude, resilience, and contentment. Their optimistic outlook allows them to navigate life's challenges with grace and find joy in the simple pleasures of everyday living.
10. Quality of Life: The Blue Zone of Costa Rica not only represents longevity but also emphasizes the importance of a high quality of life. The combination of healthy habits, strong social connections, and a sense of purpose contributes to the overall well-being and happiness of the residents.

The Blue Zone of Costa Rica stands as a living testament to the power of lifestyle and environment in promoting longevity and a fulfilling life. It is a source of inspiration, reminding us of the possibilities that exist when we prioritize our well-being and cultivate a harmonious relationship with nature and community.

So, celebrate the remarkable Blue Zone of Costa Rica, where the fountain of youth flows freely. Embrace the lessons it teaches us about nurturing our bodies, fostering meaningful connections, and finding joy in the simple pleasures of life. Let the spirit of the Blue Zone inspire you to live a long, healthy, and fulfilling life, celebrating each day as a gift in the embrace of the Nicoya Peninsula.

Caribbean Bliss: Exploring Costa Rica's Lush East Coast

Escape to the enchanting Caribbean coast of Costa Rica, where a world of tropical wonders awaits. With its lush rainforests, pristine beaches, and vibrant culture, this region invites you to immerse yourself in a blissful paradise. Join us as we embark on a journey to explore Costa Rica's lush east coast, celebrating its natural beauty, rich biodiversity, and the warm spirit of the Caribbean.

1. Tropical Paradise: The Caribbean coast of Costa Rica is a true tropical paradise, boasting some of the country's most stunning landscapes. From palm-fringed beaches to dense rainforests teeming with life, this region offers a postcard-perfect setting for your coastal escape.
2. Stunning Beaches: The Caribbean coast is renowned for its breathtaking beaches, characterized by powdery white sand and crystal-clear turquoise waters. Whether you're seeking a secluded cove for relaxation or a lively beach for water sports and socializing, the coast has it all. Playa Cocles, Puerto Viejo, and Manzanillo are just a few of the coastal gems waiting to be discovered.
3. Afro-Caribbean Culture: The Caribbean coast is home to a vibrant Afro-Caribbean culture, which infuses the region with a unique rhythm and charm. From the lively beats of reggae and calypso music to the tantalizing flavors of Caribbean cuisine, the cultural richness of the coast adds a distinctive touch to your Costa Rican experience.
4. Protected Rainforests: The Caribbean coast is adorned with protected rainforests that house an

astonishing array of flora and fauna. Explore national parks such as Cahuita National Park and Gandoca-Manzanillo Wildlife Refuge, where you can encounter monkeys, sloths, toucans, and an abundance of other fascinating wildlife species.
5. Indigenous Communities: Along the east coast, you'll have the opportunity to connect with indigenous communities such as the Bribri and Kekoldi. Learn about their ancient traditions, indigenous wisdom, and deep connection to the land. Experience their warm hospitality and appreciate the cultural diversity that makes Costa Rica such a remarkable destination.
6. Tortuguero National Park: Located on the northern Caribbean coast, Tortuguero National Park is a true gem of biodiversity and natural beauty. Accessible only by boat or plane, this protected area is a haven for nesting sea turtles, including the endangered green turtle and the iconic leatherback turtle.
7. Water Adventures: The Caribbean coast offers endless opportunities for water-based adventures. Snorkel or scuba dive in the vibrant coral reefs of Cahuita or Gandoca-Manzanillo, where you can swim alongside tropical fish, rays, and even sea turtles. Kayak through mangrove forests, exploring their intricate ecosystems and spotting unique bird species.
8. Chocolate Delights: The Caribbean coast is known for its rich history of cacao cultivation and chocolate production. Visit chocolate farms and indulge in delicious, handmade chocolate creations while learning about the traditional methods used to cultivate and process this beloved treat.
9. Surfing and Water Sports: The Caribbean coast's consistent waves and warm waters make

it a haven for surfers of all skill levels. Whether you're a seasoned pro or a beginner looking to catch your first wave, spots like Salsa Brava in Puerto Viejo offer thrilling surf experiences. Additionally, you can try paddleboarding, kayaking, or fishing in the calm waters of the coast.
10. Relaxation and Tranquility: The Caribbean coast embraces a slower pace of life, allowing you to unwind and reconnect with nature. Embrace the laid-back vibes of coastal towns like Puerto Viejo, where you can find quaint beachfront accommodations, yoga retreats, and wellness centers that promote relaxation and rejuvenation.

The Caribbean coast of Costa Rica beckons with its lush landscapes, vibrant culture, and endless opportunities for adventure and relaxation. Celebrate the blissful allure of this coastal paradise, where the warm embrace of the Caribbean meets the natural wonders of Costa Rica. Immerse yourself in the rhythms of the coast, soak in the sun-drenched beaches, and let the Caribbean spirit ignite your soul. So, set your sights on the Caribbean bliss that awaits you on Costa Rica's lush east coast. Embrace the magic of this captivating region, celebrating its natural wonders, cultural diversity, and the endless moments of pure bliss that you'll encounter along the way.

Rio Celeste: The Mystical Beauty of Costa Rica's Azure River

Nestled within the lush rainforests of Costa Rica lies a hidden gem of unparalleled beauty—the enchanting Rio Celeste. Known for its mesmerizing azure waters and ethereal surroundings, this mystical river captivates all who venture to its banks. Join us as we embark on a journey to discover the secrets and celebrate the awe-inspiring allure of Rio Celeste.

1. Natural Wonder: Rio Celeste is a true natural wonder, renowned for its unique azure color. The river's captivating hue is a result of a chemical reaction between minerals and volcanic gases, creating a sight that seems almost otherworldly.
2. Tenorio Volcano National Park: Rio Celeste flows through the heart of Tenorio Volcano National Park, adding to the park's allure and natural splendor. This protected area is a haven for biodiversity, offering visitors the chance to explore lush rainforests, volcanic formations, and breathtaking waterfalls.
3. The Legend of the Celestial Staircase: According to local folklore, the celestial beauty of Rio Celeste is said to have been created when the gods dipped their paintbrushes in the river while painting the sky. This mythical tale adds an air of mystique to the already enchanting allure of the river.
4. Hiking the Trails: Exploring the trails that wind through Tenorio Volcano National Park allows you to witness the magic of Rio Celeste up

close. Trekking along the Celeste River trail, you'll encounter captivating viewpoints, hidden waterfalls, and the iconic confluence where two rivers merge, creating the awe-inspiring azure color.

5. Waterfall of Wonders: One of the highlights of Rio Celeste is the stunning waterfall that cascades into a turquoise pool below. Witnessing the powerful rush of water and the vibrant colors blending harmoniously is a truly awe-inspiring experience that showcases the raw beauty of nature.

6. Wildlife Encounters: As you journey through Tenorio Volcano National Park and along the banks of Rio Celeste, keep an eye out for the incredible wildlife that calls this region home. Monkeys swing from the trees, vibrant birds soar overhead, and elusive jaguars and tapirs roam the dense rainforest—a testament to the rich biodiversity of Costa Rica.

7. Hot Springs and Thermal Pools: The Rio Celeste area is also home to natural hot springs and thermal pools. After a day of exploration, immerse yourself in the soothing warmth of these mineral-rich waters, allowing the healing properties to relax your body and rejuvenate your spirit.

8. Ecotourism and Conservation: The protection of Rio Celeste and its surrounding ecosystem is a testament to Costa Rica's commitment to ecotourism and conservation. The careful management of Tenorio Volcano National Park ensures that visitors can appreciate and enjoy the beauty of the river while preserving its ecological integrity for generations to come.

9. Photography and Inspiration: Rio Celeste is a photographer's dream, offering countless opportunities to capture its mystical beauty. The interplay of light, color, and nature creates a visual tapestry that ignites creativity and inspires a sense of wonder.
10. Connection with Nature: Visiting Rio Celeste allows you to disconnect from the hustle and bustle of everyday life and reconnect with the natural world. The tranquility, serenity, and sheer beauty of the river invite contemplation and a profound appreciation for the wonders that exist in Costa Rica's untouched corners.

Celebrate the mystical beauty of Rio Celeste, where the azure river weaves a spellbinding tale of nature's artistry. Embrace the sense of wonder that envelops you as you explore the ethereal landscapes, encounter exotic wildlife, and immerse yourself in the magical allure of this hidden treasure in the heart of Costa Rica. Let the mystique of Rio Celeste guide your senses and awaken your soul to the boundless marvels that await in this captivating corner of the country.

San Gerardo de Dota: Birdwatching Haven in the Cloud Forests

Discover the picturesque paradise of San Gerardo de Dota, a hidden gem nestled within the cloud forests of Costa Rica. Renowned for its exceptional birdwatching opportunities and pristine natural beauty, this charming destination offers a sanctuary for avian enthusiasts and nature lovers alike. Join us as we delve into the enchanting world of San Gerardo de Dota, celebrating its rich biodiversity, breathtaking landscapes, and the captivating allure of its feathered inhabitants.

1. Cloud Forest Splendor: San Gerardo de Dota is situated in the heart of the cloud forests, a unique ecosystem characterized by misty, moss-covered trees and a rich diversity of flora and fauna. The ethereal beauty of the cloud forests creates an enchanting backdrop for your birdwatching adventures.
2. Resplendent Quetzals: San Gerardo de Dota is considered one of the best places in Costa Rica, if not the world, to observe the magnificent resplendent quetzal. This iconic bird, with its iridescent green plumage and long, trailing tail feathers, is a symbol of beauty and grace. Witnessing the resplendent quetzal in its natural habitat is an awe-inspiring experience that is sure to leave a lasting impression.
3. Avian Richness: San Gerardo de Dota is home to an incredible variety of bird species, making it a paradise for birdwatchers. Over 170 bird species have been recorded in the area, including toucans, hummingbirds, tanagers, and

a multitude of migratory birds. The abundance of avian life ensures that every birdwatching excursion holds the promise of new and exciting encounters.

4. The Quetzal's Habitat: The cloud forests of San Gerardo de Dota provide the perfect habitat for the resplendent quetzal and other bird species. The tall trees, dense vegetation, and abundance of fruit-bearing plants create a haven for these magnificent creatures. Exploring the trails that wind through the cloud forests allows you to immerse yourself in their natural habitat and increases your chances of spotting these elusive birds.

5. Birdwatching Tours and Guides: Local guides in San Gerardo de Dota are experienced and knowledgeable when it comes to birdwatching. They can lead you to the best spots, help identify different bird species, and provide valuable insights into their behavior and ecological significance. Their expertise enhances the birdwatching experience, ensuring that you make the most of your time in this avian haven.

6. Spectacular Birding Trails: San Gerardo de Dota offers a network of well-maintained trails that wind through the cloud forests, allowing you to explore the area at your own pace. The trails provide access to different habitats and elevation levels, increasing the diversity of bird species you may encounter. Prepare to be captivated by the symphony of bird calls, the vibrant colors that flutter through the foliage, and the tranquility of the forest.

7. Natural Beauty Beyond Birds: While birdwatching is the highlight of San Gerardo de Dota, the region also boasts other natural wonders. Marvel at the cascading waterfalls, hike through the verdant forests, and breathe in the crisp, invigorating mountain air. The landscapes are a feast for the senses, inviting you to connect with nature and immerse yourself in its beauty.
8. Sustainable Tourism: San Gerardo de Dota exemplifies Costa Rica's commitment to sustainable tourism and conservation. Local communities actively participate in the preservation of the area's natural resources, ensuring that future generations can continue to enjoy the splendor of the cloud forests and the birds that call them home.
9. Lodging and Hospitality: Accommodations in San Gerardo de Dota range from cozy lodges to charming eco-retreats, all designed to blend harmoniously with the natural surroundings. The hospitality of the local communities adds a warm and welcoming touch to your stay, allowing you to feel at home amidst the tranquility of the cloud forests.
10. A Birdwatching Paradise: San Gerardo de Dota is a haven for birdwatchers, a place where time seems to stand still as you immerse yourself in the beauty of nature. Each moment spent in this avian paradise brings new discoveries, awe-inspiring encounters, and a deep appreciation for the remarkable diversity of life that thrives in the cloud forests.

Celebrate the enchanting world of San Gerardo de Dota, where the cloud forests come alive with the vibrant colors and melodic songs of its feathered residents. Embrace the sense of wonder that accompanies every sighting, and allow the magic of this birdwatching haven to ignite your passion for avian exploration and conservation. In San Gerardo de Dota, nature reveals its secrets, and the resplendent quetzal takes flight amidst a backdrop of cloud forest splendor.

Surf's Up! Riding the Waves on Costa Rica's Legendary Beaches

Welcome to the exhilarating world of surfing in Costa Rica, where legendary waves and pristine beaches combine to create a surfer's paradise. Join us as we dive into the vibrant surf culture, explore the iconic breaks, and celebrate the sheer joy of riding the waves on Costa Rica's legendary beaches. Whether you're a seasoned pro or a beginner looking to catch your first wave, the surf scene in Costa Rica promises endless excitement, breathtaking scenery, and unforgettable memories.

1. World-Class Surfing: Costa Rica is renowned worldwide for its world-class surf breaks that cater to surfers of all levels. From beginners honing their skills on gentle waves to advanced riders seeking thrilling barrels, Costa Rica offers a diverse range of surf spots to suit every surfer's preference.
2. Pacific Coast Gems: The Pacific coast of Costa Rica is dotted with legendary surf spots that have earned international acclaim. Locations such as Tamarindo, Playa Hermosa, Santa Teresa, and Pavones are just a few of the iconic beach breaks and point breaks that attract surfers from around the globe.
3. Consistent Swell: Costa Rica benefits from a consistent swell throughout the year, ensuring a steady supply of waves for surf enthusiasts. While the size and intensity may vary depending on the season, there are always waves to be ridden, making Costa Rica a year-round surfing destination.

4. Varied Wave Types: One of the beauties of surfing in Costa Rica is the diversity of wave types. From mellow beach breaks to powerful reef breaks, the country offers a range of wave conditions to suit different skill levels and preferences. Whether you're seeking long, peeling waves or fast, hollow barrels, Costa Rica has it all.
5. Surf Schools and Lessons: If you're new to surfing or looking to improve your skills, Costa Rica is an ideal place to take surf lessons. Surf schools and experienced instructors are readily available at popular surf destinations, providing guidance, safety tips, and personalized instruction to help you catch your first wave or take your surfing to the next level.
6. Vibrant Surf Culture: Surfing in Costa Rica is more than just a sport—it's a way of life. The country's vibrant surf culture is characterized by a laid-back, welcoming atmosphere that embraces both locals and visitors alike. Surf shops, beachfront cafes, and community events contribute to the sense of camaraderie and celebration that surrounds the surf scene.
7. Ecological Awareness: Costa Rica's surf community is deeply committed to environmental sustainability and the protection of the country's natural resources. Surfers actively participate in beach cleanups, marine conservation initiatives, and campaigns to raise awareness about the importance of preserving Costa Rica's coastal ecosystems.
8. Spectacular Scenery: Surfing in Costa Rica offers more than just thrilling rides—it also presents the opportunity to immerse yourself in

breathtaking natural beauty. The backdrop of lush rainforests, palm-fringed beaches, and vibrant sunsets creates a picturesque setting that enhances the surfing experience.

9. Surfing Events and Competitions: Costa Rica hosts various surfing events and competitions throughout the year, attracting professional surfers from around the world. These events showcase the country's surf talent, provide thrilling spectacles for spectators, and further solidify Costa Rica's reputation as a premier surfing destination.

10. Surf and Beyond: While surfing takes center stage, Costa Rica's legendary beaches offer an array of activities for everyone to enjoy. From yoga retreats and wellness centers to beachfront restaurants and lively nightlife, the coastal towns provide a vibrant backdrop for relaxation, exploration, and making lifelong memories.

Celebrate the thrill of riding the waves on Costa Rica's legendary beaches, where the surf culture thrives and the natural beauty is unrivaled. Whether you're a seasoned surfer seeking new challenges or a beginner taking your first steps on a board, Costa Rica's surf scene welcomes you with open arms. So paddle out, catch a wave, and experience the sheer exhilaration of surfing in this tropical paradise.

Legends and Folklore: Tales from Costa Rica's Rich Oral Tradition

Embark on a journey into the realm of legends and folklore, where the rich tapestry of Costa Rica's oral tradition comes alive. From ancient indigenous stories to tales passed down through generations, the folklore of Costa Rica is a testament to the vibrant cultural heritage of the country. Join us as we dive into the enchanting world of legends, myths, and folktales, celebrating the captivating narratives that have shaped Costa Rican culture throughout history.

1. Indigenous Mythology: Costa Rica's indigenous peoples, such as the Bribri, Boruca, and Maleku, have a deep-rooted mythology that reflects their spiritual beliefs and connection to the natural world. These indigenous legends often revolve around powerful nature deities, animal spirits, and the creation of the world, providing insights into the rich cultural heritage of these ancient communities.
2. El Cadejos: One of the most famous folktales in Costa Rican folklore is the legend of El Cadejos. This mythical creature is depicted as a large, supernatural dog with glowing eyes and shaggy fur. According to the legend, El Cadejos appears at night to protect those who are lost or in danger, while also haunting those who have committed misdeeds.
3. La Segua: La Segua is another prominent figure in Costa Rican folklore. This haunting legend tells the story of a beautiful woman who appears to men, luring them with her charm and allure.

However, those who see her true form are met with a terrifying visage of a horse's skull. La Segua is often used as a cautionary tale about the dangers of deception and vanity.

4. The Legend of the Crying Mountain: In the Talamanca region of Costa Rica, there is a legendary mountain known as Cerro de la Muerte, or the Mountain of Death. According to folklore, the mountain is said to weep tears of sorrow, particularly on misty days. The legend attributes this phenomenon to the spirits of lost souls who wander the mountain, forever seeking redemption.

5. Chirripó Grande: Chirripó Grande, the highest peak in Costa Rica, holds a special place in the folklore of the indigenous people of the Talamanca region. They believe that the mountain is a sacred dwelling place of powerful deities and ancestral spirits. Ascending Chirripó Grande is seen as a spiritual pilgrimage, allowing individuals to connect with the spiritual realm and seek guidance from the mountain's guardians.

6. The Legend of the Llorona: The legend of La Llorona, or the Weeping Woman, is widely known throughout Latin America, including Costa Rica. This tragic tale tells of a woman who, consumed by grief and guilt, wanders near rivers and lakes, crying for her lost children. La Llorona is often invoked as a cautionary figure, reminding children to listen to their parents and avoid wandering alone at night.

7. The Dancing Devils of Boruca: The Boruca people have a unique tradition that combines folklore and celebration. During their annual

"Juego de los Diablitos" (Dance of the Little Devils), participants don colorful masks and costumes to reenact the battle between the indigenous people and the Spanish conquistadors. This cultural event showcases the resilience and cultural pride of the Boruca community.

8. Oral Tradition Preservation: The folklore of Costa Rica is preserved and passed down through generations through the oral tradition. It is through storytelling, songs, dances, and community celebrations that these tales continue to thrive, connecting people to their roots and fostering a sense of cultural identity.

9. Cultural Celebrations: Costa Rica's folklore and legends are celebrated during various cultural festivals and events. These festivities showcase traditional music, dance performances, and theatrical reenactments of popular folktales. The richness of Costa Rican folklore is woven into the fabric of these celebrations, allowing locals and visitors alike to immerse themselves in the country's vibrant cultural heritage.

10. Connecting the Past and Present: Exploring the legends and folklore of Costa Rica is not only an opportunity to delve into captivating narratives but also a means of connecting with the country's past. These tales provide insights into the values, beliefs, and history of the Costa Rican people, fostering a deeper appreciation for their cultural diversity and the enduring power of storytelling.

Celebrate the captivating legends and folklore that shape Costa Rican culture, connecting the past with the present in a tapestry of enchanting narratives. Immerse yourself in the mythical realm of El Cadejos, La Segua, and the weeping mountains. Embrace the oral tradition that has kept these tales alive, and allow yourself to be transported to a world where the lines between reality and imagination blur. In Costa Rica, the legends and folklore weave a narrative tapestry that celebrates the country's cultural richness and invites you to become part of its living heritage.

Flavors of the Earth: Costa Rica's Organic Farms and Sustainable Agriculture

Step into the world of sustainable agriculture and organic farming in Costa Rica, where the bounties of the earth are cultivated with a deep respect for nature and a commitment to preserving the land for future generations. Join us as we explore the flourishing organic farms, celebrate the flavors of fresh, locally grown produce, and embrace the sustainable practices that have made Costa Rica a beacon of agricultural innovation.

1. A Sustainable Paradigm: Costa Rica has established itself as a global leader in sustainable agriculture. The country's commitment to organic farming, biodiversity conservation, and eco-friendly practices has gained international recognition and serves as a model for sustainable agricultural development worldwide.
2. Organic Certification: Organic farming in Costa Rica adheres to strict guidelines and standards set by various certification bodies. These certifications ensure that farmers employ organic practices, abstaining from the use of synthetic pesticides, genetically modified organisms (GMOs), and chemical fertilizers. Consumers can trust that organic products from Costa Rica are produced with respect for the environment and human health.
3. Biodiversity Hotspot: Costa Rica's remarkable biodiversity extends beyond its rainforests and

protected areas. Organic farms play a crucial role in preserving and enhancing biodiversity by providing habitat for native plants and animals, creating wildlife corridors, and promoting sustainable land management practices that protect delicate ecosystems.

4. Farm-to-Table Philosophy: Organic farms in Costa Rica embrace the farm-to-table philosophy, emphasizing the importance of fresh, locally grown food. By shortening the distance between the farm and the consumer, organic farmers ensure that produce is harvested at its peak, preserving its flavor, nutritional value, and reducing the carbon footprint associated with long-distance transportation.

5. Sustainable Farming Techniques: Organic farmers in Costa Rica employ a range of sustainable farming techniques to enhance soil fertility, reduce erosion, and conserve water resources. These techniques include crop rotation, companion planting, natural pest control, and the use of compost and organic fertilizers. By working with nature rather than against it, farmers cultivate healthy, resilient crops while minimizing environmental impact.

6. Agroforestry: Agroforestry is an integral part of sustainable agriculture in Costa Rica. This practice involves planting trees alongside crops, providing shade, enriching the soil, and promoting biodiversity. Agroforestry systems contribute to carbon sequestration, enhance water retention, and provide habitat for beneficial insects and birds.

7. Indigenous Wisdom: Costa Rica's indigenous communities have long practiced sustainable

agriculture, drawing on their traditional knowledge and wisdom. Organic farming in these communities integrates traditional farming methods, indigenous seeds, and cultural practices that have been passed down through generations, ensuring the preservation of cultural heritage and the promotion of sustainable livelihoods.

8. Community Supported Agriculture (CSA): Community Supported Agriculture is gaining popularity in Costa Rica, connecting consumers directly with local organic farmers. CSA programs allow individuals to subscribe to a farm's produce on a regular basis, forming a mutually beneficial relationship that supports small-scale farmers, promotes local food security, and fosters a sense of community.

9. Agrotourism: Many organic farms in Costa Rica welcome visitors and offer agrotourism experiences. These experiences allow visitors to learn about sustainable agriculture, participate in farm activities, and taste the flavors of fresh, organically grown produce. Agrotourism not only provides an opportunity for education but also directly supports the farmers and their sustainable practices.

10. Culinary Delights: The flavors of Costa Rica's organic produce are a feast for the senses. The vibrant colors, robust flavors, and nutritional richness of locally grown fruits, vegetables, herbs, and coffee beans contribute to the country's culinary excellence. Sampling these organic delights is an invitation to indulge in a gastronomic journey that celebrates the harmony between the land and the table.

11. Coffee Paradise: Costa Rica's organic farms are not limited to fruits and vegetables. The country is renowned for its high-quality, organic coffee production. The fertile volcanic soils and favorable climate create optimal conditions for coffee cultivation, resulting in rich and aromatic beans that are cherished by coffee connoisseurs around the world. Sip a cup of Costa Rican organic coffee and savor the harmonious blend of flavors and the smooth, velvety texture that only nature's finest can deliver.
12. Direct Trade and Fair Trade: Many organic farmers in Costa Rica practice direct trade or participate in fair trade initiatives. Direct trade involves establishing direct relationships between farmers and buyers, ensuring fair prices and fostering transparency. Fair trade certification further guarantees that farmers receive fair wages and work in safe conditions, empowering them to invest in their farms, communities, and sustainable practices.
13. Seed Saving and Crop Diversity: Organic farmers in Costa Rica actively participate in seed saving and the preservation of traditional crop varieties. By conserving heirloom seeds and promoting crop diversity, they safeguard genetic resources, protect against the loss of traditional knowledge, and contribute to the resilience of agricultural systems in the face of climate change.
14. Sustainable Livelihoods: Organic farming in Costa Rica not only prioritizes environmental sustainability but also supports the well-being and livelihoods of local communities. By promoting organic practices, farmers create

employment opportunities, foster economic resilience, and contribute to the development of vibrant rural communities.

15. Educational Opportunities: Organic farms in Costa Rica serve as educational platforms, offering workshops, internships, and volunteer programs that allow individuals to learn about sustainable agriculture firsthand. These opportunities inspire and empower future generations to become stewards of the land, fostering a culture of sustainability and environmental responsibility.

16. Organic Certification Programs: Costa Rica has established organic certification programs to ensure the integrity and authenticity of organic products. These programs involve rigorous inspections, audits, and adherence to organic standards, providing consumers with confidence in the organic labeling and promoting trust in the organic sector.

17. Climate Change Mitigation: Sustainable agriculture practices employed by organic farmers contribute to climate change mitigation efforts. Through carbon sequestration, reduced pesticide use, and improved soil health, organic farming plays a vital role in reducing greenhouse gas emissions and promoting climate resilience in the agricultural sector.

18. Public Support and Policy: Costa Rica's commitment to organic farming is reinforced by supportive policies and government initiatives. Public institutions provide technical assistance, research funding, and training programs to farmers, enabling them to adopt sustainable practices and further develop the organic sector.

19. Collaboration and Knowledge Sharing: Organic farmers in Costa Rica actively collaborate and share knowledge with each other, fostering a spirit of cooperation and continuous improvement. This collaborative mindset encourages innovation, the exchange of best practices, and the collective pursuit of sustainable agriculture.
20. A Greener Future: Costa Rica's organic farms represent a beacon of hope for a greener and more sustainable future. By prioritizing ecological harmony, protecting biodiversity, and promoting organic agriculture, Costa Rica paves the way for a regenerative agricultural system that nourishes both people and the planet.

Celebrate the flavors of the earth and the triumphs of sustainable agriculture in Costa Rica. Immerse yourself in the vibrant hues, tantalizing aromas, and nourishing abundance that organic farming offers. It's a journey that invites you to taste the authenticity of locally grown produce, to connect with the dedicated farmers who cultivate the land, and to appreciate the power of sustainable practices in shaping a brighter, greener tomorrow. In Costa Rica, the flavors of the earth are a testament to the harmonious relationship between agriculture and the environment, where each bite is a celebration of sustainability and the bounties of nature.

A Journey into the Canopy: Zip-lining Adventures in Costa Rica

Prepare to soar through the treetops and experience the thrill of zip-lining in the lush landscapes of Costa Rica. Join us on an exhilarating journey into the canopy, where adrenaline and awe intertwine amidst breathtaking views and an immersive natural environment. Discover why Costa Rica is renowned as one of the world's top destinations for zip-lining adventures, where the spirit of adventure meets the beauty of the rainforest.

1. Zip-lining: A Unique Perspective: Zip-lining allows you to explore the rainforest from an entirely new perspective. Suspended high above the forest floor, you'll glide through the air, propelled by gravity, and witness the magnificent beauty of the canopy up close.
2. Costa Rica: The Birthplace of Modern Zip-lining: Costa Rica holds the distinction of being the birthplace of modern zip-lining. The country's lush rainforests and towering trees provided the perfect backdrop for the development of this exhilarating activity, which has since gained popularity worldwide.
3. Safety First: Costa Rica's zip-lining industry places a strong emphasis on safety. Tour operators adhere to strict safety regulations, ensuring that participants are equipped with high-quality gear, receive comprehensive safety briefings, and are accompanied by trained guides throughout the experience.
4. Thrilling Canopy Tours: Canopy tours in Costa Rica offer a variety of zip-lining routes and

platforms, allowing you to explore different parts of the rainforest and soak in the diverse ecosystems. You'll navigate a series of suspended cables, platforms, and sky bridges, seamlessly transitioning from one exhilarating zip line to the next.

5. Breathtaking Scenery: As you zip through the canopy, be prepared to be awestruck by the breathtaking scenery that unfolds before your eyes. Lush green foliage, cascading waterfalls, and panoramic vistas of the surrounding landscapes create a visual feast that showcases the natural wonders of Costa Rica.

6. Ecological Education: Zip-lining tours in Costa Rica often include an educational component, providing insights into the country's rich biodiversity and the importance of rainforest conservation. Knowledgeable guides share information about the flora, fauna, and ecological significance of the surrounding area, enhancing the overall experience with a deeper understanding of the rainforest ecosystem.

7. Diverse Wildlife Encounters: The rainforests of Costa Rica are home to a remarkable array of wildlife, and zip-lining offers a unique opportunity to spot some of these incredible creatures in their natural habitat. Keep your eyes peeled for vibrant bird species, playful monkeys swinging through the trees, and even the occasional sighting of sloths or toucans.

8. Customizable Experiences: Zip-lining adventures in Costa Rica cater to all levels of thrill-seekers. Whether you're a first-time zip-liner or an adrenaline junkie seeking a heart-pounding adventure, there are options available to suit your preferences and comfort level. From gentle glides to exhilarating high-speed descents, the

experience can be tailored to provide the perfect balance of excitement and enjoyment.
9. Connecting with Nature: Zip-lining in Costa Rica offers a unique opportunity to connect with nature on a deeper level. The adrenaline rush combined with the peaceful serenity of the rainforest creates a sensory experience that heightens your appreciation for the natural world.
10. Environmental Sustainability: Costa Rica's zip-lining industry is committed to environmental sustainability. Tour operators implement practices that minimize their ecological impact, such as using eco-friendly materials, reforestation efforts, and supporting local conservation initiatives. By participating in zip-lining tours, you contribute to the preservation of Costa Rica's precious natural resources.
11. Multiple Zip-lining Hotspots: Costa Rica boasts numerous zip-lining hotspots throughout the country, each offering its own unique charms and landscapes. Whether you choose to soar through the Monteverde Cloud Forest, explore the Arenal Volcano region, or venture into the Osa Peninsula, you'll be treated to unforgettable zip-lining experiences in some of the most stunning locations on Earth.
12. Adrenaline and Adventure: Zip-lining in Costa Rica is not just about the views; it's an adrenaline-fueled adventure that will leave you with lifelong memories. The feeling of exhilaration as you launch yourself into the air, the wind rushing past your face, and the sheer freedom of flying among the trees create an experience that is as exhilarating as it is unforgettable.
13. An Activity for All Ages: Zip-lining is a versatile activity suitable for all ages and fitness levels. Whether you're traveling with family, friends, or

embarking on a solo adventure, zip-lining provides an inclusive and exciting experience that can be enjoyed by everyone.
14. Beyond Zip-lining: Many zip-lining tours in Costa Rica offer additional activities and amenities to enhance your experience. These may include hiking trails, canopy walks, wildlife observation points, and even opportunities for rappelling or Tarzan swings, allowing you to further immerse yourself in the beauty and adventure of the rainforest.
15. Sustainable Tourism Impact: Engaging in zip-lining adventures supports the sustainable tourism industry in Costa Rica. By choosing responsible operators who prioritize environmental stewardship and community engagement, you contribute to the local economy and the conservation efforts that make Costa Rica a global leader in sustainable tourism.

Embrace the thrill of zip-lining and embark on a journey that will take you soaring through the verdant canopies of Costa Rica. Feel the rush of adrenaline, immerse yourself in the natural wonders, and let the breathtaking landscapes leave an indelible mark on your heart. Costa Rica's zip-lining adventures offer an unparalleled fusion of adventure, nature, and exhilaration—an experience that will ignite your spirit of exploration and connect you with the true essence of this extraordinary country.

Indigenous Cultures: Celebrating Costa Rica's Native Heritage

Delve into the rich tapestry of Costa Rica's indigenous cultures, where ancient traditions and vibrant communities showcase the resilience and beauty of native heritage. Join us on a journey that celebrates the diverse indigenous groups that have inhabited these lands for centuries, honoring their wisdom, cultural practices, and contributions to Costa Rica's cultural mosaic.

1. Indigenous Diversity: Costa Rica is home to eight indigenous groups, each with its distinct language, traditions, and way of life. These groups include the Bribri, Cabécar, Maleku, Ngäbe, Huetar, Teribe, Boruca, and the Brunca people. Together, they represent a tapestry of indigenous cultures that enrich the country's cultural fabric.
2. Cultural Preservation: The indigenous communities of Costa Rica have demonstrated remarkable resilience in preserving their cultural heritage despite historical challenges. Through oral traditions, rituals, art forms, and community cohesion, they pass down their ancestral knowledge from generation to generation, ensuring the continuity of their vibrant cultures.
3. Sacred Connection to Nature: Indigenous cultures in Costa Rica share a deep-rooted connection to the natural world. They view the land, rivers, and forests as sacred, recognizing their role as stewards and caretakers of the environment. This profound relationship with

nature forms the foundation of their spiritual beliefs and sustains their harmonious way of life.
4. Traditional Arts and Crafts: Indigenous communities in Costa Rica are renowned for their exquisite craftsmanship, creating intricate handicrafts that reflect their cultural identity and connection to the natural world. From intricately woven baskets and pottery to vibrant textiles and intricate masks, these traditional arts serve as expressions of cultural pride and artistic prowess.
5. Medicinal Wisdom: Indigenous cultures in Costa Rica possess profound knowledge of traditional medicinal practices. They rely on the healing properties of native plants and herbs, using centuries-old techniques to treat ailments and maintain well-being. The wisdom of their traditional medicine continues to play a vital role in holistic healing practices today.
6. Sustainable Agricultural Practices: Indigenous communities have practiced sustainable agriculture in Costa Rica for generations. Through traditional farming methods, such as agroforestry and terracing, they cultivate crops while preserving the ecological balance of the land. These sustainable practices serve as models for ecological harmony and food security.
7. Community Values and Social Structures: Indigenous communities prioritize communal values and collective decision-making processes. Solidarity, cooperation, and mutual support are the pillars of their social structures,

fostering strong community bonds that contribute to their resilience and well-being.
8. Cultural Festivals and Celebrations: Vibrant cultural festivals and celebrations provide opportunities to witness and participate in the indigenous traditions of Costa Rica. These festivities showcase traditional music, dance performances, and theatrical reenactments of popular folktales. The richness of Costa Rican folklore is woven into the fabric of these celebrations, allowing locals and visitors alike to immerse themselves in the country's vibrant cultural heritage.
9. Indigenous Tourism: Indigenous communities in Costa Rica are embracing tourism as a means to share their cultural heritage with visitors while maintaining control over their traditions and resources. Indigenous tourism initiatives provide unique opportunities to learn from community members, participate in cultural activities, and support sustainable development within these communities.
10. Advocacy and Recognition: Costa Rica has made significant strides in recognizing and advocating for the rights of indigenous communities. The country has implemented policies that promote indigenous rights, preserve cultural heritage, and foster inclusive development. Efforts are underway to ensure that indigenous voices are heard and their contributions are acknowledged and valued.
11. Cultural Exchange and Education: Engaging in cultural exchange programs and educational initiatives allows for a deeper understanding and appreciation of indigenous cultures in Costa

Rica. By fostering respectful dialogue, learning from indigenous elders, and supporting community-led initiatives, we can cultivate a society that cherishes and celebrates the diverse cultural heritage of the country.

Celebrate the vibrant tapestry of Costa Rica's indigenous cultures, where ancient wisdom intertwines with contemporary resilience. From their sacred connection to nature to their rich traditions and artistic expressions, the indigenous communities of Costa Rica offer a window into a world where ancestral wisdom merges with a vision for a sustainable future. Through respect, understanding, and appreciation, we can honor their contributions, preserve their cultural heritage, and ensure that their vibrant traditions continue to flourish for generations to come.

Corcovado National Park: Untamed Wilderness on the Osa Peninsula

Embark on a journey into the heart of untouched wilderness as we explore the magnificent Corcovado National Park, a jewel nestled on Costa Rica's Osa Peninsula. Step into a world where biodiversity thrives, rare wildlife roams freely, and pristine landscapes beckon adventure. Discover why Corcovado is hailed as one of the most biologically diverse places on Earth, a testament to Costa Rica's commitment to conservation and the splendor of its natural treasures.

1. Natural Wonder of Biodiversity: Corcovado National Park is renowned for its exceptional biodiversity, encompassing an extraordinary array of plant and animal species. The park protects over 13 major ecosystems, including lowland rainforests, mangroves, cloud forests, and coastal habitats, creating a haven for countless species to thrive.
2. Remote and Untamed: Corcovado National Park's remote location on the Osa Peninsula has contributed to its preservation and pristine condition. Its challenging accessibility has limited human impact, allowing the park's ecosystems to remain largely undisturbed, providing a sanctuary for rare and endangered species.
3. Abundance of Wildlife: Corcovado National Park is a wildlife enthusiast's paradise, teeming with an astonishing variety of fauna. Jaguars, pumas, tapirs, and ocelots roam the dense forests, while scarlet macaws, toucans, and

parrots fill the air with vibrant colors and melodic calls. The park is also home to all four Costa Rican monkey species - the howler, spider, squirrel, and white-faced capuchin.
4. Marine Marvels: Corcovado National Park's coastal areas harbor a wealth of marine life, making it a remarkable destination for underwater exploration. Snorkelers and divers can encounter vibrant coral reefs, sea turtles, dolphins, and an abundance of tropical fish species, providing a truly immersive experience in the park's diverse ecosystems.
5. Hiking Trails: Corcovado National Park offers a network of hiking trails that wind through its lush forests, leading visitors to breathtaking waterfalls, hidden lagoons, and scenic viewpoints. Each step unveils the park's captivating beauty, allowing you to immerse yourself in the sights and sounds of an unspoiled wilderness.
6. Sirena Biological Station: The Sirena Biological Station, located within Corcovado National Park, serves as a research and educational center. Visitors can stay overnight in rustic accommodations and participate in guided tours led by knowledgeable park rangers, gaining insights into the park's ecology and conservation efforts.
7. Pristine Beaches: Corcovado National Park is blessed with pristine, untouched beaches that stretch along its coastline. These secluded strips of golden sand, bordered by dense rainforest, offer a tranquil retreat and a chance to witness nesting sea turtles during the appropriate seasons.

8. Conservation Success: The establishment of Corcovado National Park in 1975 marked a significant milestone in Costa Rica's conservation efforts. Today, the park stands as a testament to the country's commitment to protect its natural heritage and promote sustainable tourism, inspiring conservation initiatives worldwide.
9. Ecotourism Opportunities: Corcovado National Park provides unparalleled ecotourism opportunities, allowing visitors to engage in responsible and sustainable activities. Guided tours, birdwatching, wildlife spotting, and educational programs offer a chance to appreciate the park's ecological importance while supporting local communities and conservation efforts.
10. Osa Peninsula's Natural Marvels: Corcovado National Park is just one facet of the Osa Peninsula's natural marvels. The peninsula is renowned for its biological richness, boasting additional reserves, such as the Golfo Dulce Forest Reserve and Piedras Blancas National Park. Together, these protected areas form an interconnected network of biodiversity, contributing to the region's ecological significance.
11. Conservation Challenges and Continued Efforts: While Corcovado National Park celebrates its conservation successes, challenges remain in preserving its fragile ecosystems. Continued efforts are being made to combat illegal activities, promote sustainable practices, and engage local communities in conservation

initiatives to ensure the long-term protection of this invaluable natural treasure.
12. Awe-Inspiring Beauty: Corcovado National Park's awe-inspiring beauty leaves a lasting impression on all who venture into its depths. From the rhythmic sounds of the rainforest to the vibrant hues of tropical flowers, every moment spent in this untamed wilderness evokes a sense of wonder and reverence for the natural world.

Corcovado National Park on the Osa Peninsula beckons adventurers, nature enthusiasts, and conservationists to experience the raw beauty of an untouched wilderness. With its unmatched biodiversity, abundant wildlife, and pristine landscapes, the park stands as a testament to Costa Rica's dedication to preserving its natural heritage for future generations. Step into this untamed paradise and let its splendor captivate your heart, as you witness the marvels of a truly remarkable ecosystem.

Orchid Paradise: Costa Rica's Spectacular Floral Kingdom

Welcome to the enchanting realm of Costa Rica's orchids, where a breathtaking array of colors, shapes, and fragrances converge to create a floral kingdom unlike any other. In this chapter, we celebrate the diverse and magnificent orchids that grace Costa Rica's landscapes, highlighting their beauty, ecological significance, and the country's commitment to their preservation.

1. Orchid Diversity: Costa Rica is home to over 1,300 species of orchids, making it one of the most orchid-rich countries in the world. These fascinating flowers come in an astounding variety of shapes, sizes, and colors, captivating the senses with their intricate beauty.
2. Orchid Hotspots: Throughout Costa Rica, orchids thrive in various ecosystems, including cloud forests, rainforests, and highland regions. Some notable orchid hotspots include the Monteverde Cloud Forest Reserve, La Selva Biological Station, and the Osa Peninsula, where enthusiasts can witness a profusion of orchid species.
3. Ecological Significance: Orchids play a vital role in the ecosystems of Costa Rica. They provide nectar and shelter for a diverse range of pollinators, including bees, butterflies, hummingbirds, and moths. As keystone species, orchids contribute to the overall health and balance of their respective habitats.
4. Remarkable Adaptations: Orchids have evolved remarkable adaptations to attract their specific

pollinators. Some species have unique floral shapes that resemble particular insects or animals, while others emit enticing scents to lure pollinators from afar. These intricate strategies showcase the extraordinary complexity and ingenuity of nature.

5. Endemic Orchids: Costa Rica boasts numerous endemic orchid species, meaning they are found exclusively within the country's borders. These endemic orchids are a source of pride for Costa Ricans and represent the country's unique floral heritage.

6. Orchid Conservation: Recognizing the ecological and cultural significance of orchids, Costa Rica has implemented strong conservation measures to protect these delicate treasures. National parks, private reserves, and botanical gardens actively contribute to orchid conservation efforts, preserving their habitats and promoting research and education.

7. Orchid Gardens and Exhibits: Orchid gardens and exhibits provide immersive experiences for visitors, allowing them to marvel at the beauty and diversity of Costa Rica's orchids. These curated spaces showcase a variety of orchid species, offering a glimpse into the country's rich floral heritage and providing educational opportunities for orchid enthusiasts.

8. Orchid Tourism: Orchid tourism has gained popularity in Costa Rica, with specialized tours and workshops offering visitors the chance to explore orchid-rich habitats and learn from knowledgeable guides. This sustainable form of tourism supports local communities, fosters conservation efforts, and raises awareness about the importance of preserving orchid ecosystems.

9. Traditional and Medicinal Uses: Orchids have cultural significance in Costa Rica, with indigenous communities having traditional uses for some species. Additionally, certain orchids possess medicinal properties and are utilized in traditional medicine practices, highlighting their value beyond their ornamental beauty.
10. Orchid Research and Discoveries: Costa Rica continues to be a hotbed for orchid research, with ongoing discoveries and new species being documented. Scientists and botanists study the intricate relationships between orchids and their pollinators, unraveling the secrets of these captivating flowers.
11. Orchid Conservation Organizations: Several organizations in Costa Rica are dedicated to orchid conservation, research, and education. They work closely with local communities, government entities, and international partners to ensure the survival and protection of Costa Rica's orchid populations.
12. Orchids as Symbols of Beauty: Orchids are often seen as symbols of beauty, elegance, and exotic allure. Their delicate petals and intricate patterns have inspired artists, writers, and poets throughout history, capturing the imagination and igniting a sense of wonder.

Costa Rica's orchids represent a dazzling tapestry of natural beauty and botanical marvels. With their vibrant colors, alluring scents, and remarkable adaptations, these extraordinary flowers serve as a testament to the country's incredible biodiversity and its commitment to conservation. Immerse yourself in the splendor of Costa Rica's orchid paradise, and let these exquisite blooms transport you to a world of enchantment and reverence for the wonders of nature.

A Gastronomic Journey: Delving into Costa Rica's Culinary Delights

Costa Rican cuisine is a vibrant tapestry of flavors, influenced by its fertile landscapes, diverse cultural heritage, and a deep connection to the land. Embark on a mouthwatering adventure as we explore the rich culinary traditions that have made Costa Rican food a true delight for the senses. From farm-fresh ingredients to traditional recipes passed down through generations, this chapter celebrates the unique flavors and the joyful spirit of Costa Rican cuisine.

At the heart of Costa Rican cuisine is a commitment to fresh, wholesome ingredients. The fertile volcanic soil and favorable climate provide an abundance of tropical fruits, vegetables, and an array of crops. From juicy mangoes and papayas to fragrant pineapples and creamy avocados, the tropical fruits of Costa Rica add a burst of flavor and vibrancy to its culinary repertoire. These delightful fruits are not only enjoyed on their own but also incorporated into a variety of dishes, from refreshing salads to delicious smoothies.

Rice and beans are the cornerstone of Costa Rican cuisine, forming the basis of many traditional dishes. Gallo Pinto, a beloved national dish, is a delectable combination of rice and black beans sautéed with onions, garlic, and bell peppers. This savory and comforting dish is often enjoyed as part of a traditional breakfast, accompanied by eggs, tortillas, and a cup of freshly brewed Costa Rican coffee.

Speaking of coffee, Costa Rica is renowned for its exceptional coffee beans, which are grown in the fertile highland regions. The country's volcanic soil, altitude, and microclimates contribute to the production of high-quality Arabica beans, sought after by coffee connoisseurs around the world. A cup of Costa Rican coffee is a sensory experience, with its rich aroma, full-bodied flavor, and a hint of natural sweetness. Coffee plantations offer immersive tours where visitors can learn about the coffee-making process and indulge in a cup of freshly brewed perfection.

Seafood lovers are in for a treat in Costa Rica, with its long coastlines and abundant marine resources. The country's proximity to both the Pacific Ocean and the Caribbean Sea means a wide variety of fresh fish and seafood are readily available. Ceviche, a tangy and refreshing dish made with marinated raw fish or seafood, is a popular choice for those seeking a burst of tropical flavors. Freshly caught red snapper, shrimp, and tuna are often transformed into delightful ceviche creations, infused with lime juice, cilantro, and a hint of spice.

Meat lovers will find themselves indulging in succulent and flavorful dishes in Costa Rica. Traditional favorites include the mouthwatering Chifrijo, a delightful combination of crispy pork belly, black beans, rice, pico de gallo, and tortilla chips. Costa Ricans take pride in their expertly prepared meats, whether it's savory grilled chicken, tender beef, or hearty stews. Slow-cooked dishes like Olla de Carne, a comforting beef and vegetable soup, showcase the country's dedication to extracting maximum flavor from simple ingredients.

No exploration of Costa Rican cuisine would be complete without mentioning its delicious street food. Wander through bustling markets and find yourself tempted by fragrant empanadas, stuffed with savory fillings like cheese, meat, or beans. Plantains, a versatile tropical fruit, are transformed into mouthwatering dishes such as Tostones (fried plantain slices) and Maduros (ripe plantains caramelized to perfection). Costa Rica's street food scene is a testament to the country's vibrant culinary culture, where flavors burst and aromas fill the air.

For those with a sweet tooth, Costa Rica offers a delightful array of desserts and treats. The traditional Tres Leches cake, soaked in three types of milk and topped with whipped cream, is a beloved indulgence. Arroz con Leche, a creamy rice pudding infused with cinnamon and vanilla, is a comforting and nostalgic dessert often enjoyed during holidays and family gatherings. Freshly baked pastries, such as Rosquillas (crunchy and sweet cornmeal cookies) and Churros (fried dough pastries coated in sugar), provide a satisfyingly sweet conclusion to any meal.

As you explore Costa Rican cuisine, you'll discover the country's passion for preserving traditional recipes and embracing sustainable practices. Farm-to-table dining experiences offer the opportunity to savor dishes made with locally sourced ingredients, supporting local farmers and promoting a more eco-conscious approach to food.

Costa Rican cuisine is more than just food; it's a reflection of the country's vibrant culture and warm hospitality. It's an invitation to savor each bite, celebrate the simplicity of fresh flavors, and embrace the "Pura Vida" lifestyle that permeates every aspect of Costa Rican life.

Join us on this culinary journey as we celebrate the delectable delights and the colorful tapestry of flavors that make Costa Rican cuisine a true gastronomic adventure. From the simple pleasures of Gallo Pinto to the aromatic richness of Costa Rican coffee, prepare to be enchanted by the tastes and traditions that have woven their way into the heart of Costa Rican culture.

Wildlife Rehabilitation: Conservation Efforts in Costa Rica

In the heart of Costa Rica's commitment to biodiversity and environmental stewardship lies a remarkable network of wildlife rehabilitation centers. These centers, staffed by dedicated conservationists and veterinarians, play a crucial role in rescuing, rehabilitating, and releasing injured or orphaned animals back into their natural habitats. Join us as we delve into the world of wildlife rehabilitation in Costa Rica, where compassion, expertise, and a deep love for animals combine to protect and preserve the country's incredible wildlife.

1. Rescue and Rehabilitation: Wildlife rehabilitation centers in Costa Rica are on the front lines of rescuing and rehabilitating animals in need. Whether injured, orphaned, or victims of illegal wildlife trade, these centers provide essential care and treatment to ensure the animals' well-being and eventual return to the wild.
2. Species Diversity: Costa Rica's wildlife rehabilitation centers care for a wide range of species, including mammals, birds, reptiles, and even marine animals. From sloths, monkeys, and jaguars to toucans, owls, and sea turtles, these centers offer a safe haven for a remarkable diversity of wildlife.
3. Veterinary Expertise: Highly skilled veterinarians and animal care professionals work tirelessly at wildlife rehabilitation centers to provide medical treatment, surgeries, and

rehabilitation programs tailored to each species' specific needs. Their expertise is crucial in ensuring the successful recovery and release of the animals.

4. Nutritional Support: Proper nutrition is vital for the recovery of wildlife in rehabilitation. Wildlife rehabilitation centers employ specialized diets and feeding protocols to ensure that each animal receives the necessary nutrients for healing and growth. These efforts contribute to their successful rehabilitation and eventual return to the wild.

5. Enrichment and Behavioral Rehabilitation: In addition to medical care, wildlife rehabilitation centers focus on behavioral rehabilitation. Through enrichment activities, such as providing naturalistic habitats, stimulating toys, and socialization opportunities, animals regain their natural instincts and skills, preparing them for life in the wild.

6. Release and Monitoring: The ultimate goal of wildlife rehabilitation is to release animals back into their natural habitats. Once an animal has fully recovered, rehabilitation centers carefully plan and execute the release process, ensuring the best chance of survival. Monitoring programs track released animals to gather data on their adaptation and post-release success.

7. Education and Outreach: Wildlife rehabilitation centers actively engage in education and outreach programs to raise awareness about conservation, wildlife protection, and the importance of responsible interactions with wildlife. These initiatives inspire communities

and visitors to embrace their role in safeguarding Costa Rica's natural heritage.
8. Collaborative Conservation Efforts: Wildlife rehabilitation centers work closely with government agencies, conservation organizations, and local communities to create a network of support for wildlife conservation. These partnerships strengthen the impact of their efforts and foster a collective commitment to safeguarding Costa Rica's wildlife.
9. Wildlife Legislation and Enforcement: Costa Rica has enacted comprehensive wildlife protection laws and regulations to combat illegal wildlife trafficking and ensure the conservation of endangered species. Wildlife rehabilitation centers play a crucial role in supporting these laws through the rescue, rehabilitation, and release of confiscated animals.
10. Sustainable Funding: Wildlife rehabilitation centers rely on a combination of government funding, donations, grants, and volunteer support to sustain their operations. The support of individuals and organizations, both locally and internationally, is vital in maintaining the facilities, caring for the animals, and expanding conservation initiatives.
11. Success Stories: Wildlife rehabilitation centers in Costa Rica have achieved notable success in rehabilitating and releasing animals back into the wild. From the heartwarming return of rehabilitated scarlet macaws to the rescue and rehabilitation of injured sloths, each success story demonstrates the positive impact of these centers on wildlife conservation.

12. Inspiring Future Conservationists: Through their outreach programs and educational initiatives, wildlife rehabilitation centers inspire the next generation of conservationists. By fostering an appreciation for wildlife and the importance of their protection, these centers cultivate a lasting legacy of environmental stewardship in Costa Rica.

Costa Rica's wildlife rehabilitation centers embody the country's unwavering commitment to conservation. They serve as beacons of hope for injured and orphaned animals, offering them a second chance at life in the wild. These centers remind us that by working together, we can make a significant impact in preserving the rich biodiversity that makes Costa Rica a global leader in conservation.

Farewell, Costa Rica: Memories and Reflections on a Remarkable Journey

As our journey through the captivating landscapes, vibrant culture, and extraordinary biodiversity of Costa Rica comes to a close, we find ourselves reflecting on the profound impact this country has had on our hearts and souls. Costa Rica, a land of breathtaking beauty and warm hospitality, leaves an indelible mark on all who have been fortunate enough to experience its wonders. In this final chapter, we bid farewell to this remarkable country, cherishing the memories and celebrating the transformative power of our journey.

1. Natural Splendor: Costa Rica's natural splendor is unparalleled. From the mist-shrouded cloud forests and cascading waterfalls to the verdant rainforests and pristine beaches, the country's diverse landscapes inspire awe and a deep sense of connection to the natural world.
2. Pura Vida Spirit: Throughout our time in Costa Rica, we have been embraced by the Pura Vida spirit that permeates every aspect of life here. This phrase, meaning "pure life," encapsulates the country's laid-back and positive approach to life, reminding us to appreciate the simple pleasures and find joy in each moment.
3. Ecotourism Haven: Costa Rica's commitment to sustainable tourism has established it as a global leader in ecotourism. The country's extensive network of protected areas, eco-lodges, and responsible tour operators ensures that visitors

can explore its natural wonders while minimizing their impact on the environment.
4. Biodiversity Paradise: Costa Rica's unparalleled biodiversity is a testament to its dedication to conservation. From its astonishing array of bird species to its vast array of flora and fauna, the country serves as a sanctuary for countless species, making it a living laboratory for ecological study and a haven for nature enthusiasts.
5. Warmth of the People: Costa Ricans, known as Ticos and Ticas, are renowned for their warmth, friendliness, and welcoming nature. Their genuine hospitality and kind-heartedness create an atmosphere of genuine connection and leave a lasting impression on visitors.
6. Cultural Richness: Costa Rica's cultural richness is a tapestry woven from diverse influences. From the indigenous traditions to the Spanish colonial heritage and Afro-Caribbean influences, the country's cultural mosaic comes alive through its music, dance, art, and cuisine.
7. Culinary Delights: Costa Rican cuisine is a celebration of fresh, local ingredients and traditional flavors. From the beloved gallo pinto (rice and beans) to the tantalizing ceviche and mouthwatering casados (typical meals), the country's gastronomy delights the taste buds and showcases its agricultural bounty.
8. Adventures for Every Passion: Costa Rica's adventure offerings are as diverse as its landscapes. Whether zip-lining through the rainforest canopy, whitewater rafting down rushing rivers, surfing the legendary waves, or

hiking to breathtaking viewpoints, the country caters to the thrill-seeker in all of us.
9. Conservation Leadership: Costa Rica's commitment to conservation and environmental protection sets an inspiring example for the world. It abolished its military in 1948, redirecting funds towards education, healthcare, and conservation initiatives. Today, the country generates a significant portion of its energy from renewable sources and aims to be carbon neutral by 2050.
10. A Lesson in Balance: Costa Rica teaches us the importance of balance and harmony. The country's dedication to preserving its natural heritage while promoting sustainable development serves as a model for achieving a harmonious coexistence between humans and the environment.
11. Lifelong Memories: Our time in Costa Rica has left us with a treasure trove of lifelong memories. From encounters with magnificent wildlife to moments of serenity in secluded beaches, the experiences we've had in this remarkable country will forever hold a special place in our hearts.

As we bid farewell to Costa Rica, we carry with us a renewed appreciation for the splendors of the natural world, the richness of diverse cultures, and the power of conservation. The memories and reflections of our journey will continue to inspire us to be advocates for sustainability, champions of biodiversity, and ambassadors of the Pura Vida spirit. Farewell, Costa Rica, and thank you for the immeasurable gifts you have bestowed upon us. Pura Vida!

Thank you for embarking on this incredible journey through the pages of our book about Costa Rica. We hope that our words have transported you to the lush rainforests, stunning beaches, and vibrant cities of this remarkable country. Costa Rica truly is a land of wonders, and we are grateful to have shared its beauty and culture with you.

If you enjoyed reading this book and felt a sense of wonder, connection, or newfound appreciation for Costa Rica, we would be grateful if you could take a few moments to leave a positive review. Your review will not only encourage others to embark on this literary journey but also motivate us to continue sharing captivating stories and celebrating the beauty of our world.